75 birds, butterflies & little beasts

to knit and crochet

75 birds, butterflies & little beasts

to knit and crochet

Lesley Stanfield

St. Martin's Griffin
New York

75 BIRDS, BUTTERFLIES & LITTLE BEASTS
TO KNIT AND CROCHET
Copyright © 2011 Quarto, Inc. All rights reserved.
Printed in China. For information, address St. Martin's
Press, 175 Fifth Avenue, New York, N.Y. 10010.

www.stmartins.com

Library of Congress Cataloging-in-Publication Data
Available Upon Request

ISBN: 978-0-312-65605-8

First U.S. Edition: March 2011

10 9 8 7 6 5 4 3 2

Conceived, designed, and produced by
Quarto Publishing plc
The Old Brewery
6 Blundell Street
London N7 9BH

QUAR: KNCC

Project Editor: Victoria Lyle
Art Editor and Designer: Jackie Palmer
Pattern Checker: Susan Horan
Additional Designs: Jan Eaton and Caroline Sullivan
Illustrators: Coral Mula and Kuo Kang Chen
Photographer (directory and technical section): Simon Pask
Photographer (projects): Lizzie Orme
Proofreader: Liz Jones
Indexer: Richard Rosenfeld
Art Director: Caroline Guest
Creative Director: Moira Clinch
Publisher: Paul Carslake

Color separation by PICA Digital Pte Ltd, Singapore
Printed by 1010 Printing International Ltd, China

CONTENTS

FOREWORD

This is an affectionate and not entirely serious look at natural history. Somehow, translating any natural object into knitting or crochet gives it a new dimension; stylized and simplified, or cuddly and comical. It is intriguing how stitch can be used to interpret effects, ranging from the veins on a leaf to the ridges on a slug's back.

Most of the designs require an understanding of basic techniques, but some are quite easy to make and, as they are small items, only small amounts of yarn are needed.

Feel free to experiment, and reward yourself, your family, and friends with your knitting and crochet skills.

LESLEY STANFIELD

ABOUT THIS BOOK

This book provides an enchanting selection of over 75 birds, butterflies, and little beasts for you to knit and crochet, as well as designs for stunning flowers and plants. Each and every one of these gorgeous creations can be used to embellish garments, gifts, accessories, and much more.

SECTION 1: BEFORE YOU BEGIN
(PAGES 8–21)

The book begins with some basic knitting and crochet information about yarns, needles and hooks, symbols, abbreviations, and terminology, as well as some notes on how to work the key stitches featured in the book – much of the know-how you need to get started.

SECTION 2: DIRECTORY
(PAGES 22–43)

The Directory is a showcase of the 75 beautiful designs that feature in this book. Flick through this colorful visual guide, select your design, and then turn to the relevant page of instructions to create your chosen piece.

Each design is shown in proportion to the others on the spread, which gives an idea of size and scale.

Each item is labeled with a number that corresponds to the relevant instructions in the Instructions chapter (pages 44–109).

SECTION 3: INSTRUCTIONS
(PAGES 44–109)

Organized into separate knitting and crochet sections, here you'll find instructions on how to create every design featured in the Directory. The majority of the crochet designs are explained with charts as well as written instructions. This is so that you can use either method or, better still, combine both. Unfortunately, there isn't space to include charts for some of the larger and three-dimensional designs, but care has been taken to present all the instructions as clearly as possible.

All knitted and crocheted designs have a symbol indicating the pattern's degree of difficulty: basic, intermediate, or advanced.

LEVEL OF DIFFICULTY

	Knitting	Crochet

Each design is accompanied by a symbol indicating the pattern's degree of difficulty:

Basic

Intermediate

Advanced

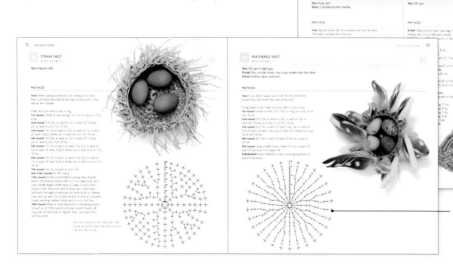

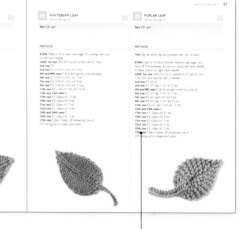

In the crochet section, charts are provided for the majority of the designs to amplify the instructions.

Full instructions are provided for each knitted and crochet design.

SECTION 4: PROJECTS
(PAGES 110–125)

The beauty of these designs is that they can all be used to embellish a number of items, from garments and accessories, to the table and walls of your home. This chapter presents a selection of ideas to inspire and encourage you to use the featured designs in a variety of ways.

PROJECT 4: CORAL NECKLACE

Jumbo-sized knitted coral and outsize fake pearl beads are a frivolous take on traditional jewelry, although finer yarn could be used for a daintier result. Using a sharp-pointed needle, the coral and beads were strung on strong thread, and the ends stitched to organza ribbon, folded in the middle.

Each project is illustrated with a photograph of the finished item.

A close-up photograph of each project shows in detail how the item has been made and put together.

BEFORE YOU BEGIN

Before you get started, here is some useful information about yarns, needles, hooks, symbols, and abbreviations, as well as some notes to help you brush up on your knitting or crochet skills.

MATERIALS AND EQUIPMENT

Few materials and minimal craft skills are needed for the designs featured in this book. Obviously, changing the type of yarn and color will produce a different result and scale, so it can be very rewarding to experiment.

YARNS

Yarns are available in a range of weights, from 3ply to extra chunky. Because yarns may vary from one manufacturer to another and certainly change from one fiber to another, only generic yarn types are indicated in this book—although smooth yarns are recommended for crochet—and no needle or hook sizes are given. You should be aware of the properties of different yarns, however, from the fullness of cotton to the elasticity of wool, because the construction of a yarn will affect its behaviour and characteristics, and so will influence the end result. Experimentation is key. Try using different tensions and, if in doubt, use a smaller needle/hook size than usual.

If you really want to create a florist's shop (or a greengrocer's counter!) separate your yarns into color groups and keep these in transparent plastic containers so that you have a palette of colors to work with. Don't limit yourself to knitting yarn and look for interesting colors among embroidery threads.

KNITTING NEEDLES

As already mentioned, no needle sizes are specified in this book, but you will want to vary your choice of needle depending on the yarn you are using. Pairs of knitting needles are made in a variety of lengths. Most are aluminum, although larger-size needles are made of plastic to reduce their weight. For most of the designs in this book, a conventional pair of needles is used, but two double-pointed needles are needed to make a cord, and four double-pointed needles where there is knitting in the round. Bamboo needles are available in many sizes.

A variety of different yarn types and weights.

CROCHET HOOKS

Crochet hooks are available in a wide range of sizes and materials. Most hooks are made from aluminum or plastic. Small sizes of steel hooks are made for working with very fine yarns. Handmade wooden, bamboo, and horn hooks are also available.

Hook sizes are quoted differently in Europe and the United States, and some brands of hook are labeled with more than one numbering system. Choosing a hook is largely a matter of personal preference. The design of the hook affects the ease of working considerably. Look for a hook that has a comfortable grip.

Pairs of knitting needles and double-pointed needles in various materials and sizes.

ADDITIONAL EQUIPMENT

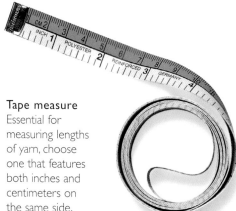

Tape measure
Essential for measuring lengths of yarn, choose one that features both inches and centimeters on the same side.

Markers and row counters
Readymade markers can be used to indicate a repeat or to help count stitches in a chain (see page 20 for the use of yarn markers). Similarly, a row counter may help you to keep track of the number of rows you have worked, but in knitting this is usually easy if you remember to include the stitches on the needle as a row.

Scissors
Choose a small, sharp-pointed pair to cut yarn and trim yarn ends.

CROCHET SYMBOLS
KEY TO SYMBOLS USED IN CHARTS

BASIC SYMBOLS

◯ Slip ring

◯ Chain

● Slip stitch

+ Single crochet

┬ Half double

┬ Double

┬ Treble

┬ Double treble

⌣ Work in the single front strand of the stitch below – this concave curve will appear underneath the stitch symbol, for example: slip stitch in front strand of stitch below.

⌣·

∩ Work in the single back strand of the stitch below – this convex curve will appear underneath the stitch symbol, for example: single crochet in back strand of stitch below.

⟩ An arrowhead indicates the beginning of a row or round where this is not immediately apparent.

INCREASES

Symbols joined at the base show stitches worked in a single stitch or space to make an increase. They are usually described as "work so many stitches in the next stitch," or at the beginning of a row "work so many stitches in the stitch below."

 2-st sc increase

 2-st dc increase

 3-st dc increase

 2-st tr increase

 3-st tr increase

DECREASES

Symbols joined at the top show stitches gathered into one stitch to form a decrease. Each stitch of the group (tr, dtr, etc., according to the symbol) is made without working the last wrap (a wrap is yarn round hook, then pull yarn through loop). This leaves one loop on the hook for each incomplete stitch plus the original loop. The decrease is completed by taking the yarn round the hook and then pulling the yarn through all loops on the hook.

 2-st sc decrease

 2-st dc decrease

 3-st dc decrease

 2-st tr decrease

 tr and dtr decrease

WRAPS

A wrap is yarn round hook, then pull yarn through loop (see above its use in decreasing). In color changing, working the last wrap of a stitch with the new color makes a neat change-over.

CLUSTERS

A cluster is made exactly like a decrease (see left) except that the stitches are all worked in a single stitch or space before being gathered together at the top.

 2-st dc cluster

 3-st dc cluster

 2-st tr cluster

 3-st tr cluster

POPCORNS

A popcorn is worked in one stitch like a cluster (see above), but the stitches are gathered together differently at the top. Each popcorn is explained in the instructions.

 4-st tr popcorn

ABBREVIATIONS

KNITTING ABBREVIATIONS

k	knit
kfb	knit in front and back of stitch to make two stitches from one
m1	make a stitch by lifting strand between stitches from front and knit in back of strand
m1L	as m1, noting that new stitch slants to the left
m1p	make a stitch by lifting strand between stitches from front and purl in back of strand
m1R	make a stitch by lifting strand between stitches from back and knit in front of it to make a stitch that slants to the right
p	purl
pfb	purl in front and back of stitch to make two stitches from one
RS	right side(s)
skpo	slip one stitch knitwise, knit one, pass slipped stitch over (this is an alternative to ssk below)
ssk	slip two stitches one at a time knitwise, insert point of left-hand needle into the fronts of these two stitches and knit them together (this is an alternative to skpo above)
ssp	slip first stitch knitwise, then slip second stitch knitwise, return stitches to left-hand needle, take right-hand needle round to purl both stitches together through back loops
s2kpo	slip two stitches as if to knit two together, knit one, pass the slipped stitches over
sk2po	slip one knitwise, knit two together, pass slipped stitch over
st(s)	stitch(es)
st-st	stockinette stitch
tbl	through the back of the loop(s)
tog	together
wyab	with yarn at back
wyif	with yarn in front
WS	wrong side(s)
yo	yarn forward and over needle to make a stitch

CROCHET ABBREVIATIONS

ch	chain
ch sp	chain space
dec	decrease
dc	double
dtr	double treble
hdc	half double
RS	right side(s)
sc	single crochet
sp	space
ss	slip stitch
st(s)	stitch(es)
tr	treble
trtr	triple treble
WS	wrong side(s)
yrh	yarn round hook

KNITTING AND CROCHET

[ ]	work instructions in square brackets the number of times stated
( )	round brackets indicate a group of stitches to be worked in one place
* **	asterisks mark a section of instructions to be repeated

TERMINOLOGY AND AFTERCARE

ENGLISH/AMERICAN TERMINOLOGY

The patterns in this book use American terminology, which differs somewhat from English terminology. You may find this list of American terms and their English equivalents useful.

AMERICAN	ENGLISH
single crochet (**sc**)	double crochet (**dc**)
half double crochet (**hdc**)	half treble (**htr**)
double crochet (**dc**)	treble (**tr**)
treble (**tr**)	double treble (**dtr**)
double treble (**dtr**)	triple treble (**trtr**)

AFTERCARE

It is a good idea to keep a ball band from each project you complete as a reference for washing instructions, or alternatively make a note of them. Standard laundering symbols are given below, although you may prefer to wash your knitted or crocheted item by hand. If so, this should be done gently in hot water, with a mild, detergent-free cleaning agent. Most purpose-made wool or fabric shampoos are ideal, but check the one you choose does not contain optical brighteners which will cause yarn colors to fade. Always rinse the piece thoroughly and allow it to dry naturally.

STANDARD LAUNDERING SYMBOLS

Hand Washing

Do not wash by hand or machine

Hand washable in warm water at the stated temperature

Machine Washing

86°F / 30°C

Machine washable in warm water at the stated temperature

86°F / 30°C

Machine washable in warm water at the stated temperature, cool rinse and short spin

104°F / 40°C

Machine washable in warm water at the stated temperature, short spin

Bleaching

Bleaching not permitted

CL

Bleaching permitted (with chlorine)

Pressing

Do not press

Press with a cool iron

Press with a warm iron

Press with a hot iron

Dry Cleaning

Do not dry clean

A

May be dry cleaned with all solutions

P

May be dry cleaned with perchlorethylene or fluorocarbon- or petroleum-based solvents

F

May be dry cleaned with fluorocarbon- or petroleum-based solvents only

NOTES ON KNITTING

This section is not a lesson in knitting; it is simply a reminder of a few basics, together with a few suggestions and techniques that might be new to an inexperienced knitter.

SLIPKNOT

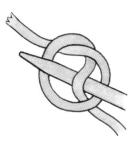

1 Putting a slipknot on the needle makes the first stitch of the cast-on. Loop the yarn around two fingers of the left hand, the ball end on top. Dip the needle into the loop, catch the ball end of the yarn, and pull it through the loop.

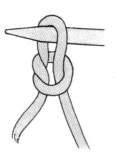

2 Pull the ends of the yarn to tighten the knot. Tighten the ball end to bring the knot up to the needle.

CASTING ON

There are several cast-on methods, each with their own merits.

THUMB METHOD

Sometimes called long-tail cast-on, this uses a single needle and produces an elastic edge.

1 Leaving an end about three times the length of the required cast-on, put a slipknot on the needle. Holding the yarn end in the left hand, take the left thumb under the yarn and upward. Insert the needle in the loop made on the thumb.

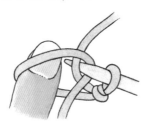

2 Use the ball end of the yarn to make a knit stitch, slipping the loop off the thumb. Pull the yarn end to close the stitch up to the needle. Continue making stitches in this way. The result looks like a row of garter stitch because the yarn has been knitted off the thumb.

CABLE CAST-ON

This two-needle method gives a firm edge with the appearance of a rope.

1 Put a slipknot on one needle. Use the other needle and the ball end of the yarn to knit into the loop on the left-hand needle without slipping it off. Transfer the new stitch to the left-hand needle.

2 Insert the right-hand needle between the new stitch and the next stitch, and then make another stitch as before. Continue making stitches in this way.

KNITTED CAST-ON

Make a cable cast-on as above, but instead of knitting between stitches, insert the right-hand needle in the front of each stitch in the usual way. This gives a softer edge than the cable method.

CORD

A very useful round cord can be made using two double-pointed needles.

Cast on three (or the required number of) stitches and knit one row in the usual way. * Without turning, slide the stitches to the opposite end of the needle. Take the yarn firmly across the wrong side from left to right and knit one row. Repeat from * for the required length.

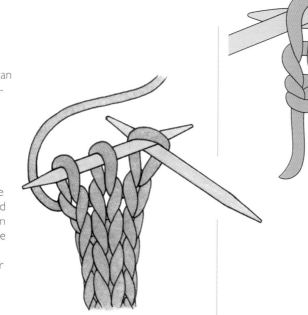

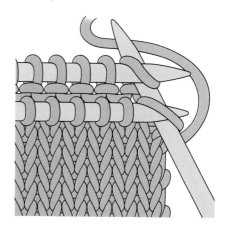

CHAIN

Put a slipknot on the needle. * Knit one stitch. Transfer the stitch just made from the right-hand to the left-hand needle. Repeat from * for the length required. A similar fine chain can be made using a wool needle and starting in the last stitch of a cast-off. Bring the yarn end through the stitch from back to front. Loop the yarn. Insert the needle in the stitch loop from front to back and then in the new loop from back to front. Continue in this way, making loops from left to right and right to left alternately.

BINDING OFF

CHAIN BIND-OFF

A simple knit stitch bind-off is used in most of these projects. Knit two stitches. * With the left-hand needle, lift the first stitch over the second. Knit the next stitch. Repeat from * until one stitch remains. Break the yarn, take the end through this stitch, and tighten.

When a row is only partially bound off, the count of stitches to be worked usually includes the stitch already on the needle.

PICOT BIND-OFF

In a decorative picot bind-off additional stitches are cast on, then these are bound off, followed by one or more stitches of the last row. The stitch remaining from the bound-off is slipped on to the left-hand needle ready to make the next cast-on. Obviously, the number of stitches bound off must exceed the number of stitches cast on, but both can be varied. The closer the picots are spaced, the more the edge will flute. In the illustration, two stitches have been cast on and four stitches bound off.

BINDING OFF TWO SETS OF STITCHES TOGETHER

The two sets of stitches are held on parallel needles, right sides or wrong sides together according to the instructions. A third needle is used to knit together the first stitch from each needle, and then the next pair. The first stitch made on the third needle is taken over the second stitch in the same way as for a chain bind-off. Continue to knit together pairs of stitches and bind them off along the row. This joins edges in a very neat, flexible way.

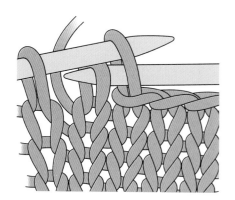

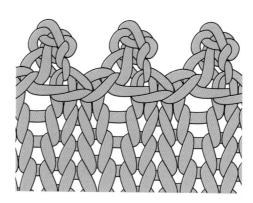

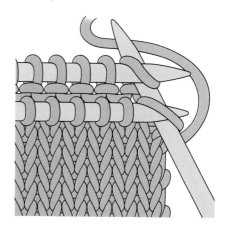

NOTES ON CROCHET

Understanding how to make simple stitches is the key to constructing interesting shapes in crochet. Here are a few reminders of some basics and some suggestions for building on them.

SLIPKNOT

1 Putting a slipknot on the hook makes the first loop of the chain that will hold the stitches of the first row or round. Loop the yarn around two fingers of the left hand, the ball end to the front. Insert the hook in the loop, catch the ball end of the yarn, and pull it through the loop.

2 Pull the ends of yarn to tighten the knot. Now tighten the ball end to bring the knot up to the hook.

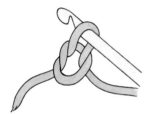

HOOKING ACTION

Hold the slipknot (and later the chain) between the thumb and forefinger of the left hand. Take the yarn over the second finger of the left hand so it is held taut. Take it around the little finger as well if necessary. The right hand is then free to manipulate the hook. With a turn of the wrist, guide the tip of the hook under the yarn. Catch the yarn and pull it through the loop on the hook to make a chain.

Hooking and catching is referred to as yarn round hook (abbreviation: yrh). It is the action used in making a chain, a slip stitch and, in various combinations, all other crochet stitches.

Note Unless the instructions state otherwise, the hook should be inserted under the two strands of yarn which form the top of the chain, or the top of the stitch.

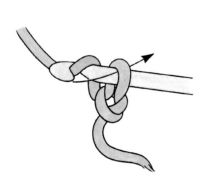

ROUNDS

Rounds are started in a chain ring, or in a slip ring for a tighter center, and are worked in an counterclockwise direction without turning over.

CHAIN RING

Join a number of chain stitches into a ring with a slip stitch in the first chain. Work the first round of stitches around the chain and into the center. If the yarn end is also worked around, the ring is lightly padded and this end can be pulled to tighten it.

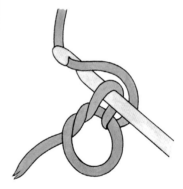

SLIP RING

1 To make a slip ring, first coil the yarn around two fingers and then use the hook to pull through a loop of the ball end of the yarn, as if making a slipknot (see step 1, above left). However, do not then pull the yarn tight. Holding the ring flat between the thumb and forefinger of the left hand, catch the yarn and pull it through the loop on the hook to anchor it.

2 Working under two strands of yarn each time, make the stitches as directed and then pull the free yarn end to close the ring. Join the ring with a slip stitch in the first stitch.

ROWS

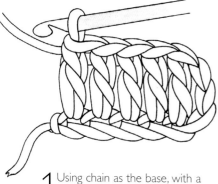

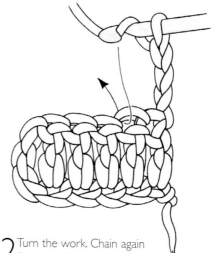

1 Using chain as the base, with a stated number of chain nearest the hook forming the first stitch, work a stitch in each subsequent chain from right to left. The illustration shows a first row of double crochet, with three chain as the first stitch.

2 Turn the work. Chain again forms the first stitch of the next row, but be careful to make the second stitch in the right place. It should go into the next stitch of the previous row and not into the stitch immediately below. Working into the stitch below is the equivalent of making two stitches in the same stitch and results in an increase.

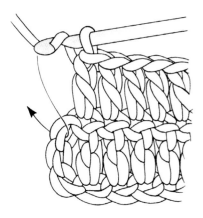

3 The last stitch of this row is made in the top chain of the three chain forming the first stitch of the previous row.

Note Crochet stitches are not symmetrical, as the chain that forms the top of the stitch lies to one side of the main part of the stitch (see the illustrations of rows of doubles above). As a beginner, you may find this disconcerting when first working in rows. Rounds are easier to understand because the stitches all lie in the same direction, usually on the right side of the crochet.

INVISIBLE FASTENING OFF

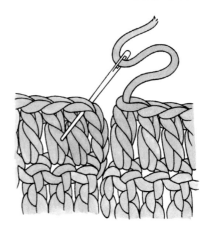

1 For a smooth finish to an edging round, simply break the yarn (leaving an end long enough to sew with) and pull it through the loop of the last stitch. Thread it on to a wool needle and take the needle under the two strands of the first stitch.

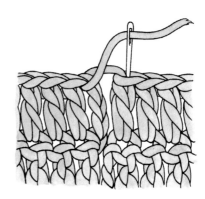

2 Then take it back into the last stitch to form a new stitch, or alternatively pull it tight until it disappears. Fasten off by darning in the yarn end along the chain edge.

ADDITIONAL KNOW-HOW

MARKERS

If markers are needed to count rows or repeats, use a length of contrast thread. * Lay it between stitches from front to back, make a stitch and then bring it from back to front of the work. Repeat from * once. It can be pulled out when it is no longer needed.

NEEDLES AND HOOKS

Use a size smaller than usual for all these projects. If particularly small needles or hooks are required, this will be indicated in the instructions.

KNITTING TIPS

If the yarn snarls, hold the working end of the yarn and, leaving the needle in place, suspend the work so that it spins until the kinks have been unwound.

With small projects especially, it is often more convenient to leave stitches on hold on a length of contrast yarn rather than a spare needle. This way there is no weight to distort the stitches.

Ssk and skpo (see Abbreviations, page 14) are both methods of making a decrease with the top stitch sloping to the left, and one can be substituted for the other, according to preference.

When knitting in the round with double-pointed needles, the stitches are worked off the left-hand needle and on to the right-hand (free) needle in the usual way. This is done with the right side (the outside) facing, unless stated otherwise. Take the yarn firmly from one double-pointed needle to the next or a ladder will appear.

"Wrap and turn" is explained where it is used. It is simply a method of avoiding a hole when making a mid-row turn. Taking the yarn around the stitch next to the turn anchors the first stitch of the turned row, but it must be done firmly to minimize the blip caused.

CROCHET TIPS

Yarn markers (see left) can be used as an aid to counting rows in crochet, just as in knitting. But they are especially useful for marking the beginning/end of rounds. To do this, the yarn is taken from one side of the work to the other vertically between rounds, instead of horizontally between stitches.

Rounds are worked in a counterclockwise direction, usually with the right side facing.

It is frustrating to find that a yarn in the color you want to use is too bulky for crochet, so try splitting it. This can be done as you go along—but experiment first to check that the yarn will withstand this treatment. It may be fine for these small projects but this is not recommended for garments. Otherwise, stranded tapestry yarn is the answer.

These are two methods of making nice round cords by slip stitching into chain. 1. With the flat, V-shaped front of the chain toward you, miss one chain, then slip stitch under two strands of each chain. 2. Ignore the V-shaped strands, miss one chain, then slip stitch into the single looped strand at the back of each chain. Each chain has a slightly different character.

MAKING UP

PRESSING

It's important to pin out flat projects, such as leaves, wrong side uppermost, and damp press if the yarn is suitable—or dry press otherwise. This can greatly enhance the shape and character of the project. Three-dimensional items are shaped by stuffing, but even so, a very light press on the right side after completion will smooth the surface and seams.

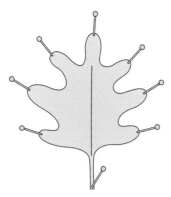

ENDS

Sometimes called a tail, the end of yarn left after making the slipknot should be a reasonable length so that it can be used for sewing up. It can also be very useful for covering up imperfections, such as awkward color changes. The same applies to the end left after binding off. In these projects, ends left at the tips of petals or leaves will be better darned in before the main making up.

EMBROIDERY

To make spots on butterfly wings, make a short stitch over a single strand of yarn and, if necessary, pad it with a second stitch over the first.

Use "invisible" nylon thread to sew on sequins and matching sewing thread for beads. Beads are best anchored with a back stitch. To sew on sequins for fish scales, start at the tail end and, alternating sequins on each row, overlap them as you stitch. Overlapping them more closely will give a truly scaly effect but will add weight.

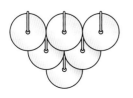

SEAMS

As explained under Ends (see left), yarn ends are immensely useful for making up. But if a new length of yarn needs to be joined, start with a back stitch rather than a knot. Unless stated otherwise, invisible seaming on the right side (see below) is recommended for most projects, including crochet. To avoid bulk, take in only half a stitch from each edge when seaming crochet.

INVISIBLE SEAMING

The neatest way to seam is to use mattress (or ladder) stitch. With right sides facing and starting at the cast-on, take the wool needle under the strand between the first and second stitches of one edge. Repeat at the other edge. Continue working into alternate edges, tightening the stitches as you go, to close up an invisible join.

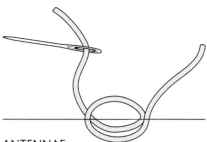

ANTENNAE

Insert the wool needle at the position of the first antenna, leaving a yarn end. Bring the needle out at the position of the second, back stitch between the two, then bring the yarn out again at the second. Trim both ends. Stiffen them by pinning out straight and spraying with a fabric stiffener or strong hairspray. Leave to dry.

STUFFING

Use synthetic filling (batting) rather than cotton wool, as the latter can be rather dense and difficult to stitch through. Push the batting in firmly, one wisp at a time, using it to shape the object without distorting it. Too much batting will pack down whereas too little will never plump up. Don't push the batting in with a pointed implement, but use something like the eraser end of a pencil. Spare matching yarn may be better than batting inside crochet, as there will be no show-through. Wind off short lengths of yarn around two fingers and push these in, one coil at a time.

WIRING

Some items need a little help to stay in shape, and wiring is the solution. Fine, soft wire such as fuse wire is suitable for the snail's horns, for example (see page 100), and can be threaded on to a needle and inserted that way. Where stronger wire is needed, be careful not to leave a burr when snipping it, as this will make it difficult to insert. A small file, even an old nail file, can be used to smooth away a burr.

DIRECTORY

Featured here is a varied collection of birds, bees, butterflies, flowers, fruit, and vegetables in knitting and crochet. Look through this section to find the design you want, then turn to the Instructions for the description of how to make it.

SPRING THINGS

From the first few flowers to the hatching of eggs, spring is a season full of promise. It's also a time to enjoy tender colors and to be creative with knitting and crochet.

3 EASTER EGGS

55 PRIMULA

4 GRAY NEST

36 PIGEON FEATHER

37 HEN'S EGG

55 PRIMULA

3 EASTER EGGS

38 STRAW NEST

39 FEATHERED NEST

HEDGEROW FLOWERS

The vibrant pinks and yellows of wild flowers are complemented by the blues of insects and a single little bird. The round Blue Tit stands sturdily among the leaves and flowers.

51 BACHELOR'S BUTTON

50 EAR OF WHEAT

52 FOXGLOVE

1 BLUE TIT

18 ELDER LEAF

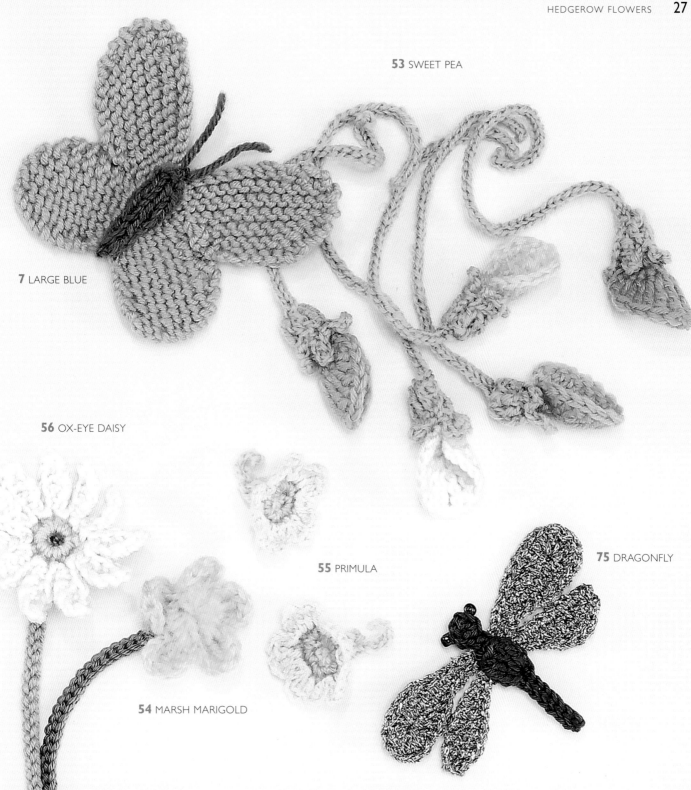

53 SWEET PEA

7 LARGE BLUE

56 OX-EYE DAISY

55 PRIMULA

75 DRAGONFLY

54 MARSH MARIGOLD

LEAF FALL

Who hasn't admired the variety of shapes, the detail and the fresh colors of leaves? Capture some of this in stitch and use the result for appliqué decoration and trimmings.

60 STRAWBERRY LEAF

18 ELDER LEAF

23 POPLAR LEAF

21 BEECH LEAF

20 ELM LEAF

57 CLOVER LEAF

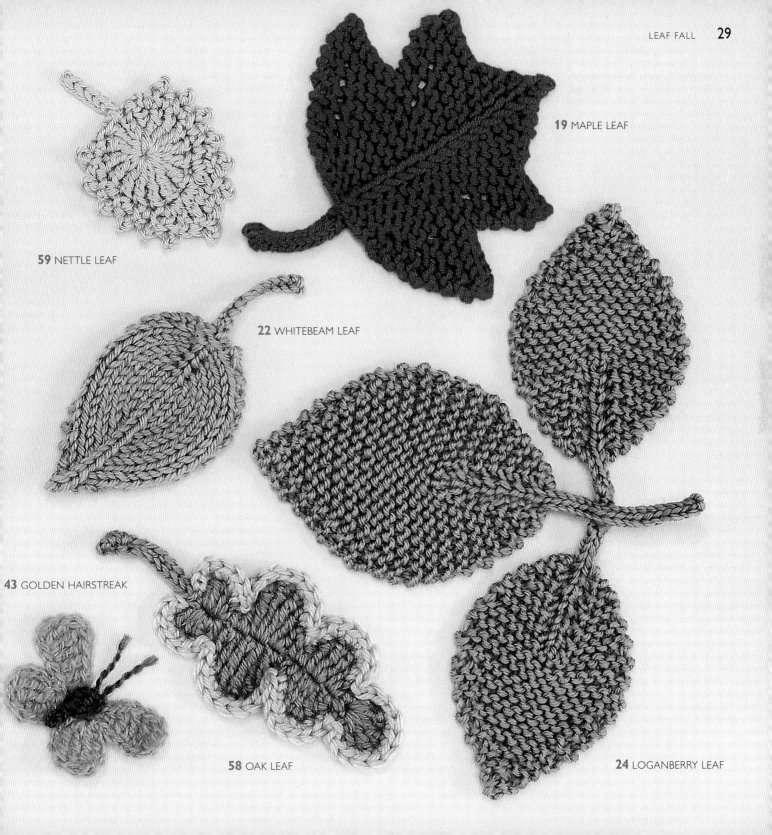

19 MAPLE LEAF

59 NETTLE LEAF

22 WHITEBEAM LEAF

43 GOLDEN HAIRSTREAK

58 OAK LEAF

24 LOGANBERRY LEAF

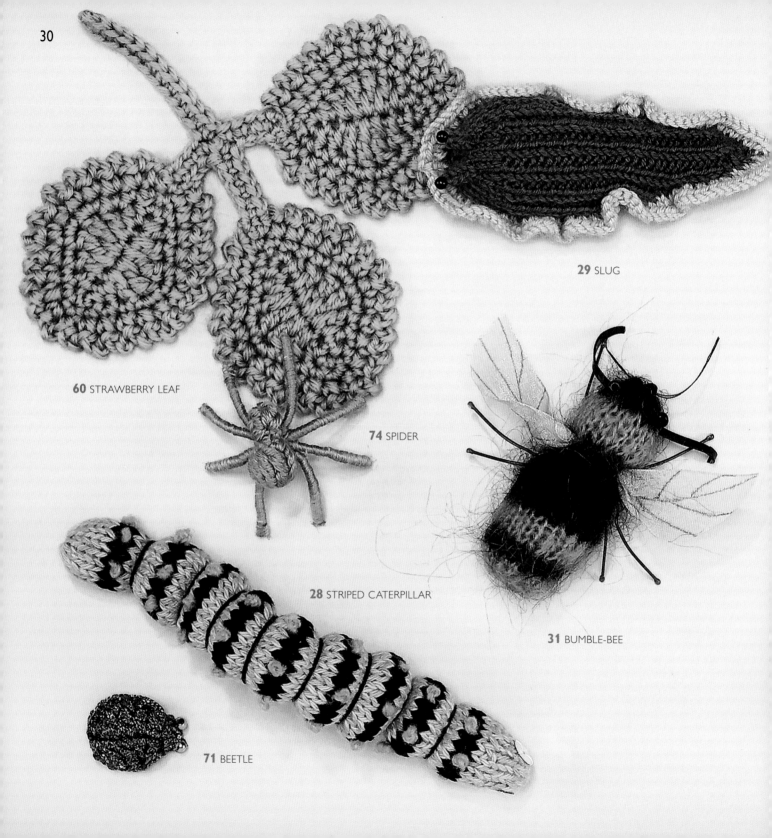

29 SLUG

60 STRAWBERRY LEAF

74 SPIDER

28 STRIPED CATERPILLAR

31 BUMBLE-BEE

71 BEETLE

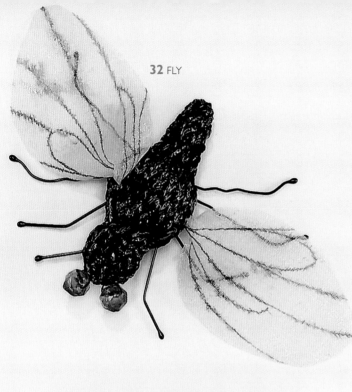

32 FLY

BUGS AND BEASTIES

Charming to some people, but obnoxious to others, creepy crawlies become quite harmless, even comical, when they're soft and woolly. A few have sharp ingredients but they're mostly user-friendly.

24 LOGANBERRY LEAF

72 LADYBUG

73 FURRY CATERPILLAR

70 SNAIL

30 HONEY-BEE

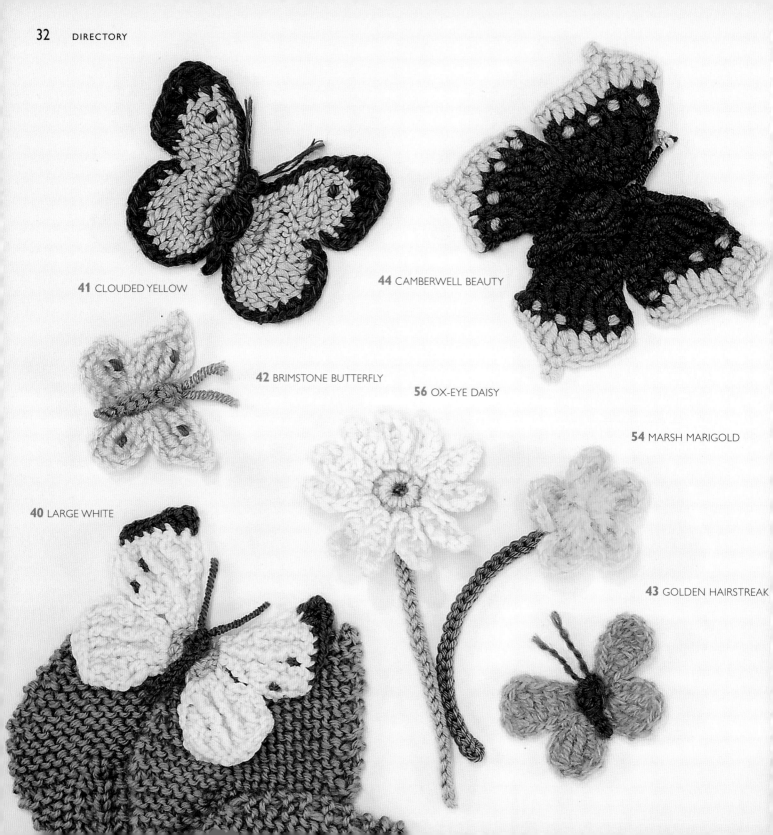

41 CLOUDED YELLOW

44 CAMBERWELL BEAUTY

42 BRIMSTONE BUTTERFLY

56 OX-EYE DAISY

54 MARSH MARIGOLD

40 LARGE WHITE

43 GOLDEN HAIRSTREAK

6 PEACOCK BUTTERFLY

9 FRITILLARY

8 COMMON BLUE

7 LARGE BLUE

BUTTERFLIES

Take to the air with a cloud of brilliant butterflies. They range from easy-to-make to more advanced, and from fairly realistic to very stylized. Their colors could be varied to create other species.

ROCK POOL

The seashore is a treasure trove of inspiration for knitting and crochet. From the shiny scales of fish to the soft tendrils of seaweed, lots of effects can be captured with the right colors and textures.

11 FAN SEAWEED

14 SPRAT

47 GOLDFISH

49 BRANCHING SEAWEED

45 PEBBLES

48 SEA ANEMONE

13 STARFISH

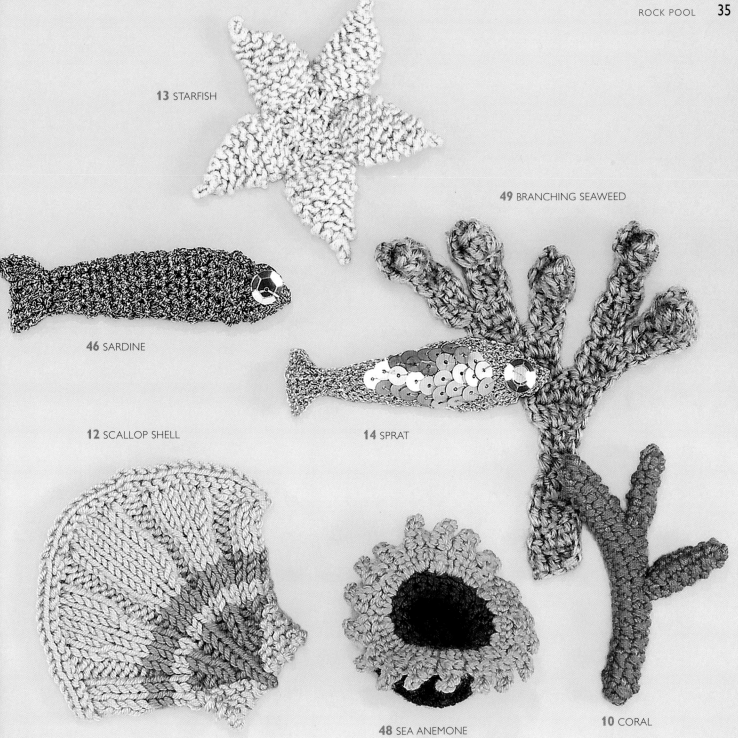

13 STARFISH

49 BRANCHING SEAWEED

46 SARDINE

12 SCALLOP SHELL

14 SPRAT

48 SEA ANEMONE

10 CORAL

62 LIME AND LEAF

63 OLIVES

72 LADYBUG

24 LOGANBERRY LEAF

25 LOGANBERRY

66 CHILI

61 STRAWBERRY

60 STRAWBERRY LEAF

42 BRIMSTONE BUTTERFLY

FRUIT BOWL

No wonder tiny insects are attracted to these luscious leaves and fruit! Beads stud the loganberries and strawberries in a jewel-like way and the sections of lemon and apple look good enough to eat!

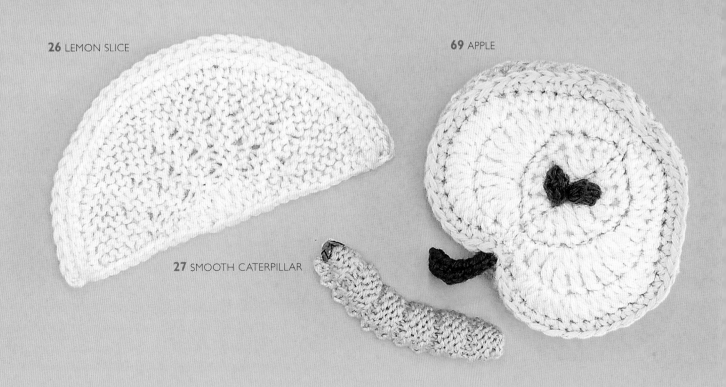

26 LEMON SLICE

69 APPLE

27 SMOOTH CATERPILLAR

63 OLIVES

27 SMOOTH CATERPILLAR

VEGETABLE BASKET

An end-of-season collection of tactile, curvaceous vegetables is a harvest festival in stitches. The little snail is as at home here as he would be adorning a hat or a bag.

64 RED BELL PEPPER

67 YELLOW SQUASH

65 CORN

72 LADYBUG

68 STRIPED SQUASH

70 SNAIL

29 SLUG

35 FLY AGARIC

58 OAK LEAF

76 CEP MUSHROOM

33 ACORN

WOODLAND WALK

Gathering mushrooms and collecting fall leaves is something you can do all the year round with these designs. Use warm, rich colors to capture the mood.

19 MAPLE LEAF

70 SNAIL

74 SPIDER

77 WAXCAP

34 FIELD MUSHROOM

17 HOLLY LEAF AND BERRIES

2 DOVE

79 LARGE SNOWFLAKE

16 MISTLETOE

78 CHRISTMAS STAR

16 MISTLETOE

79 SMALL SNOWFLAKE

MIDWINTER

Handmade decorations and gift-wrap trims make celebration and present-giving very special. From the white dove to the twinkling star, there's something for every Christmas here.

15 CHRISTMAS ROSE

17 HOLLY LEAF AND BERRIES

INSTRUCTIONS

Organized into knitting and crochet, this chapter contains
full instructions on how to create all of the designs
featured in the book, including charts for the majority
of the crochet designs. It also provides photographs of
the individual designs from a variety of angles for easy
reference and additional visual information.

KNITTED DESIGNS

SEE ALSO

Knitting Abbreviations: page 14

Notes on Knitting: pages 16–17

Additional Know-How: pages 20–21

BLUE TIT
directory view page 26

Yarn Yarn 4-ply yarn in white (A), blue (B), black (C), olive (D), and yellow (E)
Extras 4 double-pointed needles, batting, 2 black beads, soft wire for jewelry making, small pliers (optional)

METHOD

Note Each time a turn is made mid-row the wrap-and-turn technique should be used to prevent a hole: before turning, take the yarn to the opposite side of the work, slip the next st purlwise from the left-hand needle to the right-hand needle, return the yarn to the original side of the work, slip the st back on to left-hand needle, turn, tension the yarn ready to make the first st.

HEAD Using 2 needles and A, cast on 2 sts.
1st row (RS) K1, m1, k1. 3 sts.
2nd row P.
3rd row K1, [m1, k1] twice. 5 sts. Break off A, change to B.
4th and WS rows P.
5th row K1, [m1, k1] 4 times. 9 sts.
7th row K1, m1, k7, m1, k1. 11 sts.
9th row K9, turn, p7, turn, k6, turn, p5, turn, k to end.
11th row K1, k2tog, k5, ssk, k1. 9 sts.
13th row K1, k2tog, s2kpo, ssk, k1. 5 sts.

14th row P. Break off B.
15th row RS facing and starting at cast-on edge, using first double-pointed needle and A, pick up and k3 sts from A row ends and 9 sts from B row ends, with 2nd double-pointed needle work (k2tog, k1, ssk) across 5 sts, with 3rd double-pointed needle pick up and k9 sts from B row ends and 3 sts from A row ends. 27 sts. Now turn and work in rows with 4 double-pointed needles:
1st row (WS) P. Break off A.
2nd row Using C, k. Break off C.
3rd row Slip first 2 sts of row on to spare yarn. Using separate lengths of yarn, join A and p next 9 sts, using C p next 5 sts, using A p next 9 sts, slip last 2 sts on to spare yarn. Turn and continue with 23 sts on needles. Cross yarns at each color change on next 6 rows.
4th row K9A, (k1, m1, k3, m1, k1)B, k9A. 25 sts.
5th row P9A, 7C, 9A.
6th row K9A, 7C, 9A.
7th row P8A, 9C, 8A.
8th row K7A, 11C, 7A.
9th row P6A, 13C, 6A. Break off A and C, continue with D.
BACK 10th row K8, m1, [k3, m1] 3 times, k8. 29 sts.
11th and WS rows P.
12th row K.
14th row [K2tog] twice, k7, [m1, k7] twice, [ssk] twice. 27 sts.
16th row [K2tog] twice, k6, m1, k7, m1, k6, [ssk] twice. 25 sts.
18th row [K2tog] twice, k5, m1, k7, m1, k5, [ssk] twice. 23 sts. Continue to decrease and increase in this way on RS rows, working one st less beside each double decrease, until 26th

row has been completed and 15 sts remain.

28th row [K2tog] twice, m1, k7, m1, [ssk] twice. 13 sts.

30th row [K2tog] twice, k5, [ssk] twice. 9 sts.

32nd row K2tog, k5, ssk. 7 sts. Break off D and continue with B.

TAIL ** P1 row.

1st rib row (RS) K2, [p1, k1] twice, k1.

2nd rib row K1, [p1, k1] 3 times. Repeat these 2 rows 3 times more, then work 1st rib row again. Bind off knitwise.

FRONT RS facing, slip 4 remaining sts of head on to needle and rejoin C to work bib.

1st row [K2tog] twice. 2 sts.

2nd and WS rows P.

3rd row K1, m1, k1. 3 sts.

5th row K1, [m1, k1] twice. 5 sts.

7th row K1, m1, k3, m1, k1. 7 sts. Break off C and continue with E.

Beginning with a p row, work 3 rows st-st.

11th row K1, [m1, k1] 6 times. 13 sts.

13th row K1, m1, k to last st, m1, k1. 15 sts.

15th row As 13th row. 17 sts.

17th row K to last 2 sts, turn, p to last 2 sts, turn, k to last 3 sts, turn, p to last 3 sts, turn, k to end.

19th row As 13th row. 19 sts.

21st row As 17th row.

23rd row As 13th row. 21 sts.

25th row As 17th row.

27th row Ssk, k3, ssk, k7, k2tog, k3, k2tog. 17 sts.

29th row Ssk, k2, ssk, k5, k2tog, k2, k2tog. 13 sts.

31st row Ssk, k1, ssk, s2kpo, k2tog, k1, k2tog. 7 sts. Break off E and continue with B.

TAIL As tail of back from **.

WING TIPS RS facing and using D, starting at first decrease along edge of left back, pick up

and k19 sts. Change to B. P 1 row.

2nd row (RS) K2, [p1, k1] 7 times, turn, rib 13, turn, rib 11, turn, rib 9, turn, rib to end. Bind off knitwise. Work 2nd wing tip to match.

BEAK Using C, cast on 5 sts.

Single row (RS) K1, s2kpo, k1. Draw yarn through remaining 3 sts and pull tight.

FINISHING Head: turn to WS to carefully fasten off ends. On RS, join edges of C rows of bib to A row ends and neaten A sts around cast-on group above. Stuff head then, joining cast-on edge into a ring, sew beak to top of bib. Neaten ends of wing tips and, starting at head, join back and front, stuffing as you stitch. Close body at tail end and on RS join both tail pieces by back stitching through both layers just inside the edge sts. Sew on beads for eyes. Cut a length of wire— approximately 18in (45cm)—and using fingers or pliers, leave an end to form an upright in the bird's body and then bend the wire to form 4 toes (see Diagram 1). Take the wire along the leg, making a 90° bend where the top of the leg is to be. Insert the long remaining length of wire through the body to exit where the 2nd leg is to be and, at the same time, bury the first upright in the body above the first leg. Bend the long end into a leg to match the first and trim the excess to make a 2nd upright to go inside the body (Diagram 2). Using C, bind the legs and feet, without covering the claws. At the top of the legs, bind further with E.

Note This bird should not be used as a toy, but it could be made without legs and with French knots for eyes to make it safe for young children.

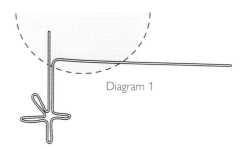

Diagram 1

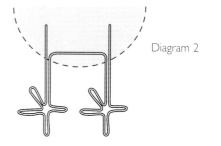

Diagram 2

2 DOVE
directory view page 42

Yarn 4-ply yarn in pink (A) and white (B)
Extras 4 double-pointed needles, batting, 2 small red beads

METHOD

Note Each time a turn is made mid-row the wrap-and-turn technique should be used to prevent a hole: before turning, take the yarn to the opposite side of the work, slip the next st purlwise from the left-hand needle to the right-hand needle, return the yarn to the original side of the work, slip the st back on to left-hand needle, turn, tension the yarn ready to make the first st.

Using pair of needles and A, cast on 2 sts.
1st row (RS) Kfb, k1. 3 sts.
2nd and 4th rows P.
3rd row K1, [m1, k1] twice. 5 sts.
5th row K.

6th row P. Change to B.
7th row K1, [m1, k1] 4 times. 9 sts.
8th row P.
9th row K2, m1, [k1, m1] 5 times, k2. 15 sts.
10th row P1, m1p, p to last st, m1p, p1. 17 sts.
11th row K1, m1, k14, turn, p13, turn, k11, turn, p9, turn, k7, turn, p5, turn, k10, m1, k1. 19 sts.
12th row As 10th row. 21 sts.
13th row K1, m1, k1, [ssk] 4 times, k1, [k2tog] 4 times, k1, m1, k1. 15 sts.
Change to double-pointed needles, putting 5 sts on each of 3 needles and marking the beginning of each round (see page 20).
1st round (RS) K.
2nd round [K1, m1] 3 times, k2, ssk, k1, k2tog, k2, [m1, k1] 3 times. 19 sts.
K 2 rounds.
5th round K1, m1, [k2, m1] 3 times, k5, [m1, k2] 3 times, m1, k1. 27 sts.
K 3 rounds.
9th round K1, m1, [k2, m1] 3 times, k13, [m1, k2] 3 times, m1, k1. 35 sts.
K 3 rounds.
13th round K1, m1, [k2, m1] 5 times, k13, [m1, k2] 5 times, m1, k1. 47 sts.
K 8 rounds.
22nd round K7, ssk, [k2, ssk] twice, k13, [k2tog, k2] twice, k2tog, k7. 41 sts.
K 2 rounds.
25th round K7, ssk, [k1, ssk] twice, k11, [k2tog, k1] twice, k2tog, k7. 35 sts.
K 2 rounds.
28th round K7, [ssk] 3 times, k9, [k2tog] 3 times, k7. 29 sts.
K 2 rounds.
31st round K5, [ssk] 3 times, k7, [k2tog] 3 times, k5. 23 sts.
K 2 rounds.
34th round K1, [ssk] 4 times, k5, [k2tog] 4 times, k1. 15 sts.
Close underside of head and beak. Insert batting, lightly filling head but shaping body firmly.

35th round K1, [p1, k1] 6 times, p2tog. 14 sts.
36th round [K1, p1] to end.
37th round [K1, pfb] 7 times. 21 sts.
38th round [K1, p2] to end.
39th round [K1, p1, m1, p1] 7 times. 28 sts.
40th, 41st, and 42nd rounds As 36th round.
43rd round [K1, pfb] 14 times. 42 sts.
44th, 45th, 46th, 47th, and 48th rounds As 38th round.
Picot bind-off * Cast on 2 sts by knitted cast-on method
(see page 16), bind off 3 sts, slip remaining st from right-
hand needle to left-hand needle; repeat from * to last st.
Fasten off.
WINGS (make 2)
Using pair of needles and B, cast on 37 sts.
1st row (RS) P1, [k1, p1] to end.
2nd row K1, [p1, k1] to end.
3rd row Rib 35, turn, rib 33, turn, rib 31, turn, rib 29, turn,
rib 27, turn, rib 25, turn, rib to end.
4th row As 2nd row.
Picot bind-off as before.
FINISHING Fold wings in half and join along inside of picot
bind-off. Flatten tail and join in the same way. Position wings
along line of shaping on each side of back. Oversew along
top edge of wing, working into each p st of rib, then sew
underside to match, catching down the end of the wing.
Sew on beads for eyes.

3 EASTER EGGS
directory view page 24

Yarn DK yarn for larger egg (6¼in/16cm circumference), 4-ply yarn for smaller egg
(5in/12.5cm circumference)—note, an elastic yarn such as pure wool is essential.
Needles 4 double-pointed needles, two sizes smaller than usual for the yarn
Extra Egg molds (from craft stores)

METHOD

Cast on 3 sts on one needle.
Foundation row (RS) [Kfb] 3 times. 6 sts.
Without twisting, put 2 sts on each of 3 needles. With RS
facing and using 4 needles, continue in rounds of k. Use
contrast yarn to mark the end of each round (see page 20).
1st round [Kfb] 6 times. 12 sts.
2nd and alternate rounds K.
3rd round [K2, m1] 6 times. 18 sts.
5th round [K2, m1] 9 times. 27 sts.
7th round [K3, m1] 9 times. 36 sts. K 16 rounds. Use end
at base to neaten the joining round, then fasten it off on
the inside.
24th round [K4, k2tog] 6 times. 30 sts. K 4 rounds.
29th round [K3, k2tog] 6 times. 24 sts. K 2 rounds.
32nd round [K2tog] 12 times. 12 sts. Slip sts on to contrast
yarn and insert mold, rounder end first. Replace sts on
3 needles.
33rd round [K2tog] 6 times. 6 sts. Pull out marker yarn. Break
main yarn and take it through remaining 6 sts in the direction
of work. Fasten off firmly.

4 GRAY NEST

directory view page 24

Yarn DK yarn in dark gray (A) and light gray (B)
Needles 2 pairs, one pair a size smaller than the other

METHOD

Using larger needles and A, cast on 4 sts.
1st row (RS) [Kfb] 4 times. 8 sts.
2nd and WS rows P.
3rd row [Kfb] 8 times. 16 sts.
5th row [Kfb] 16 times. 32 sts.
7th row [K1, make 10-st chain in next st (see page 17), drop chain st, wyif slip next 5 sts purlwise, wyab put chain st on to left-hand needle then k this st, k next st] 4 times.
9th row [K1, kfb, k2] 8 times. 40 sts.
11th row As [ ] of 7th row 5 times.
13th row [K2, kfb, k2] 8 times. 48 sts.
15th row As [ ] of 7th row 6 times.
17th row [K2, kfb, k3] 8 times. 56 sts.
19th row As [ ] of 7th row 7 times.
21st row K.
23rd row As 19th row. Continue with smaller-size needles and B.
25th, 26th, and 27th rows K.
Beginning with a p row, work 5 rows st-st.
33rd row [K5, k2tog] 8 times. 48 sts. Work 3 rows st-st.

37th row [K4, k2tog] 8 times. 40 sts.
Work 3 rows st-st.
41st row [K3, k2tog] 8 times. 32 sts.
P one row.
43rd row [K2tog] 16 times. 16 sts. P one row.
45th row [K2tog] 8 times. 8 sts.
46th row [P2tog] 4 times. Fasten off by running end of yarn through remaining 4 sts.
FINISHING Join seam with ladder st on RS (see page 21). Tug chain loops and press lightly. With light gray lining turned in, use B to slightly gather top by running a thread around inside of edge sts.

5 SWANSDOWN

directory view page 25

Yarn DK yarn (preferably with a multistrand construction)
Needles Small-size knitting needles, yarn needle

METHOD

Single loop * K one st without slipping it off, bring yarn between needles to front, take yarn under and over left thumb, then back between needles, ** k st remaining on left-hand needle, drop loop, slip 2nd st on right-hand needle over first st.
Double loop Taking yarn under and over left thumb twice, work as single loop from * to **, then, again taking yarn around thumb twice, repeat from * to **; k st remaining on left-hand needle, slip 2nd and 3rd sts on right-hand needle over first st.
Triple loop Taking yarn around left thumb twice, work as single loop from * to **, then, again taking yarn around thumb twice, repeat from * to ** twice; k st remaining on left-hand needle, slip 2nd, 3rd, and 4th sts on right-hand needle over first st.

Make a 6-st chain (see page 17) and, without turning, slip last st back on to left-hand needle. Using the knitted cast-on method (see page 16), cast on 16 sts. 17 sts.
Loop row Make 3 single loops, 4 double loops, 3 triple loops, 4 double loops, 3 single loops. Slipping first st, bind off purlwise. Fasten off, leaving a long end.

6 PEACOCK BUTTERFLY
directory view page 33

Yarn DK yarn in buff (A), rust (B), blue (C), yellow (D), and black (E)
Needles 3 knitting needles

METHOD

RIGHT LOWER WING Using A, cast on one st.
1st row (RS) (K1, yo, kfb) in one st. 4 sts.
2nd row P.
3rd row [Kfb, k1] twice. 6 sts.
4th row Pfb, p3, pfb, p1. 8 sts.
5th row K2, k2tog, [yo] 3 times, ssk, k2. 9 sts.
6th row P3, (k1, p1, k1) in triple yo, p3. **
7th row Ssk, k7. 8 sts.
8th row P6, ssp. 7 sts.
9th row Ssk, k5. 6 sts.
10th row P4, ssp. 5 sts. Bind off knitwise.
LEFT LOWER WING Using A, work as right lower wing to **.
7th row K7, k2tog. 8 sts.
8th row P2tog, p6. 7 sts.
9th row K5, k2tog. 6 sts.
10th row P2tog, p4. 5 sts. Bind off knitwise.
RIGHT UPPER WING Using B, work as right lower wing to **.
7th row K.
8th row P.
9th row K7, k2tog. 8 sts.
10th and 12th rows P.
11th row K6, k2tog. 7 sts.
13th row Change to A, k5, k2tog. 6 sts.
14th row Ssp, p4. 5 sts.
15th row K5, along straight row-ends of right lower wing, RS facing, pick up and k6 sts. 11 sts. Leave sts on a spare needle.
LEFT UPPER WING Using B, work as right lower wing to **.
7th row K.
8th row P.
9th row Ssk, k7. 8 sts.
10th and 12th rows P.
11th row Ssk, k6. 7 sts.
13th row Change to A, ssk, k5. 6 sts.
14th row P4, ssp. 5 sts.

15th row Break yarn. With RS facing, pick up and k6 sts along straight row-ends of left lower wing, k across 5 sts of left upper wing. 11 sts. Do not break yarn. With RS together, place both sets of sts on parallel needles and, using 3rd needle, bind them off together knitwise (see page 17).
BODY Using A, cast on 10 sts.
Single row (RS) (K1, yo, k1) in first st, turn, k3, turn, slip 2nd and 3rd sts over first, k this st tbl. Bind off knitwise.
FINISHING Press wings to shape. Fasten off ends, working a few sts over first cast-on st of each wing. Using C for lower wings and D for upper wings, make a ring of running st around eyelets, then overcast these edges. Outline overcast sts with a ring of backstitch in E. Catch down edges of lower wings underneath upper wings. Sew body in place. Using A, split yarn and make antennae (see page 21).

FINISHING With cast-on edge facing, fold loop row so that chain remains free. Using long end and taking in one strand from each edge, join pairs of cast-on sts with overcasting. Turn over and join bound-off sts with backstitch. Fasten off first end by taking yarn through each st of chain to counteract any curve in the chain. Cut each loop at the halfway point. Trim lower loops and then use yarn needle to fray out all ends of yarn.

7 LARGE BLUE
directory view page 27

Yarn DK yarn in pale blue (A) and deep blue (B)
Needles 3 knitting needles

METHOD

RIGHT LOWER WING Using A, cast on 4 sts.
1st row (RS) K2, kfb, k1. 5 sts.
2nd and WS rows K.
3rd row Kfb, k2, kfb, k1. 7 sts.
5th row K5, kfb, k1. 8 sts.
7th row K6, kfb, k1. 9 sts.
8th row K. Break yarn and leave sts on a spare needle.
LEFT LOWER WING Using A, cast on 4 sts.
1st row (RS) Kfb, k3. 5 sts.
2nd and WS rows K.
3rd row Kfb, k2, kfb, k1. 7 sts.
5th row Kfb, k6. 8 sts.
7th row Kfb, k7. 9 sts.
8th row K. Break yarn and, both RS facing, slip sts of right lower wing on to left-hand needle. 18 sts.
9th row K.
11th row K1, k2tog, k to last 3 sts, k2tog, k1. 16 sts.
13th row As 11th row. 14 sts.
15th row K1, k2tog, k2, [k2tog] twice, k2, k2tog, k1. 10 sts.
17th row K1, [k2tog] 4 times, k1. 6 sts.
18th row K. Break yarn and leave sts on a spare needle.
RIGHT UPPER WING Using A, cast on 6 sts.
1st row (RS) Kfb, k3, kfb, k1. 8 sts.
2nd row Kfb, k7. 9 sts.
3rd row Kfb, k6, kfb, k1. 11 sts.
4th row Kfb, k10. 12 sts. Break yarn and leave sts on a spare needle.
LEFT UPPER WING Using A, cast on 6 sts.
1st row (RS) Kfb, k3, kfb, k1. 8 sts.
2nd row K6, kfb, k1. 9 sts.
3rd row Kfb, k6, kfb, k1. 11 sts.
4th row K9, kfb, k1. 12 sts. Break yarn and leave sts on a spare needle.

Joining row All RS facing, across sts of right upper wing work kfb, k11; across sts of lower wings work k1, [k2tog] twice, k1; across sts of left upper wing work k10, kfb, k1. 30 sts.
6th row K.
7th row Kfb, k12, [k2tog] twice, k11, kfb, k1.
8th row K.
9th row K13, [k2tog] twice, k13. 28 sts.
10th row K.
11th row K1, k2tog, k9, [k2tog] twice, k9, k2tog, k1. 24 sts.
12th row Bind off knitwise, working k1, k2tog, k18, k2tog, k1 across the row.
BODY Using B, cast on one st.
1st row (RS) (K1, yo, k1) in this one st. 3 sts.
2nd row P1, p1tbl, p1.
3rd row K1, [yo, k1] twice. 5 sts.
4th row P1, [p1tbl, p1] twice.
5th row K.
6th row P. Repeat last 2 rows.
9th row K2tog, k1, skpo. 3 sts.
10th row P.
11th row K.
12th row P.
13th row S2kpo. Fasten off remaining one st.
FINISHING Press to shape. Lightly gather center of butterfly vertically to measure slightly less than the length of the body. Attach body. Pinch upper and lower wings together, upper over lower, and hold with a few sts on WS. Using B, add antennae (see page 21).

8 COMMON BLUE
directory view page 33

Yarn 4-ply yarn in mid blue (A) and deep blue (B)
Needles 3 knitting needles

METHOD

LOWER WING Lower wing (make 2) Using A, cast on 12 sts.
1st row (RS) K2, [p2, k1] 3 times, k1.
2nd row K1, [p1, k2] 3 times, p1, k1.
3rd row K2, [p2tog, k1] 3 times, k1. 9 sts.
4th row K1, [p1, k1] 4 times.
5th row K1, sk2po, p1. sk2po, k1. 5 sts.
6th row K1, [p1, k1] twice.
7th row K1, sk2po, k1. 3 sts. Break yarn and leave sts on a spare needle.
UPPER WING (make 2) Using A, cast on 12 sts.
1st row (RS) K2, [p2, k1] 3 times, k1.
2nd row K1, [p1, k2] 3 times, p1, k1. Repeat 1st and 2nd rows once.
5th row K2, [p2tog, k1] 3 times, k1. 9 sts.
6th row K1, [p1, k1] 4 times.
7th row K2, [p1, k1] 3 times, k1.
8th row As 6th row.
9th row K1, sk2po, p1, sk2po, k1. 5 sts.
10th row K1, [p1, k1] twice.
11th row K1, sk2po, k1. 3 sts. Break yarn and leave sts on a spare needle.
BODY Using B, cast on 6 sts by cable method (see page 16). Bind off knitwise.
FINISHING Join wings: RS together, line up the pair of upper wings and the pair of lower wings on 2 needles, then use 3rd needle to bind them off together knitwise (see page 17). Press wings lightly. With yarn ends to the top, stitch body to wings, then use ends to make antennae (see page 21).

FRITILLARY
directory view page 33

Yarn DK yarn in brown (A) and orange (B)
Needles 2 pairs of knitting needles,
one a size smaller than the other

METHOD

WINGS Using larger needles and A, cast on 3 sts.
1st row (RS) [Kfb] twice, k1. 5 sts.
2nd row [Pfb] 4 times, p1. 9 sts.
3rd row [Kfb] 8 times, k1. 17 sts.
Note On next and every rib row work all k sts on RS and all p sts on WS through the back of the loop.
4th row (WS) K1, [p1, k1] 8 times.
5th row P1, [k1, pfb] 7 times, k1, p1. 24 sts.
Continue with B.
6th row K1, [p1, k2] 7 times, p1, k1.
7th row P1, [k1, p1, m1, p1, k1, p2] 3 times, k1, p1, m1, p1, k1, p1. 28 sts.
8th row [K1, p1] 3 times, * k2, [p1, k1] twice, p1, repeat from * twice, k1.
9th and 10th rows K all k sts and p all p sts as they appear.
11th row P1, [k1, p1, inc2, p1, k1, p2] 3 times, k1, p1, inc2, p1, k1, p1. 36 sts.
12th row [K1, p1] 4 times, k2, * [p1, k1] 3 times, p1, k2; repeat from * once, [p1, k1] 4 times.
13th and 14th rows As 9th and 10th rows.
FIRST WING TIP ** ** Next row (RS) P1, k1, [pfb, k1] 3 times, p1, turn. Continue on these 12 sts.
2nd row K1, p1, [k2, p1] 3 times, k1.
3rd row K2tog, [p2, k1] twice, p2, ssk. 10 sts. Fasten off and leave sts on spare yarn. ***

SECOND WING TIP RS facing, rejoin yarn to first of remaining sts. Work as first wing tip from ** to ***.
THIRD AND FOURTH WING TIPS As second wing tip.
BINDING OFF WING TIPS WS facing, slip sts of first wing tip on to needle. Using smaller size needles and A, working all bound-off sts knitwise, bind off one st, * slip st on to left-hand needle, cast on one st, bind off 3 sts; repeat from * to end.
Work remaining wing tips to match.
WING EDGING RS facing, using smaller-size needles and A, pick up and k 12 sts along side edge of first wing.
Bind off knitwise. Edge fourth wing to match.
BODY Using larger-size needles and A, cast on 2 sts.
K1 row, p1 row.
3rd row (RS) K1, m1, k1. 3 sts. P1 row.
5th row K1, [m1, k1] twice. 5 sts. St-st 3 rows.
9th row K1, m1, k3, m1, k1. 7 sts. St-st 5 rows.
15th row K1, ssk, k1, k2tog, k1. 5 sts. P1 row.
17th row K1, s2kpo, k1. 3 sts. P1 row.
19th row S2kpo. Fasten off remaining one st.
FINISHING Gather center top of wings. Around wing tips use A to neaten corners. Use A to make a spot between each rib near the bound-off edge (make spot with 2 small sts over one strand of A). Seam body and stitch in place. Make antennae (see page 21).

Specific abbreviation **inc2** (k1tbl, k1) in next st, then insert tip of left-hand needle behind the vertical strand that runs down between the 2 sts just made and k this tbl to make 3rd st of group.

10 CORAL
directory view page 35

Yarn DK cotton
Needles 3 double-pointed needles
Extra Pipe cleaner

METHOD

MAIN STEM Using double-pointed needles, cast on 6 sts.
* **1st row** (RS) [K1, p1] 3 times. Without turning, slide sts to opposite end of needle, take yarn firmly across back of work.
2nd row (RS) [P1, k1] 3 times. Without turning, slide sts to opposite end of needle, take yarn firmly across back of work. **
These 2 rows form pattern (seed st). Repeat from * to ** 6 times more.
FIRST BRANCH Do not turn, cast on 6 sts by knitted cast-on method (see page 16). Do not turn, continue on these 6 sts only:
1st row (RS) [K1, p1] 3 times. Without turning, slide sts to opposite end of needle, take yarn firmly across back of work.
2nd row Using 3rd double-pointed needle and leaving 6 sts of main stem on left-hand needle: [p1, k1] 3 times. Without turning, slide sts to opposite end of needle, take yarn firmly across back of work. Repeat these 2 rows 3 times more. Turn, (WS facing), bind off these 6 sts in pattern. Fasten off. Turn to RS and rejoin yarn to 6 sts of main stem. Pattern 8 rows as before.
SECOND BRANCH Cast on 4 sts by knitted cast-on method. Do not turn, continue on these 4 sts only. Using 3rd needle and leaving 6 sts of main stem on left-hand needle as before, pattern 4 rows. Turn, (WS facing), bind off these 4 sts in pattern. Fasten off. Turn to RS and rejoin yarn to 6 sts of main stem. Pattern 8 rows. Turn and bind off as before.
FINISHING From the top, insert pipe cleaner into 2nd branch and a little way into main stem. Trim pipe cleaner at the top. Do the same with first branch. Insert pipe cleaner in main stem and trim. Use ends of yarn to firm joins at base of branches and to close main stem and branches. If the strand at the back forms a ladder, back stitch over this to look like moss st.

11 FAN SEAWEED
directory view page 34

Yarn 4-ply yarn

METHOD

Note The seaweed is worked from the top.

Cast on 55 sts by the thumb method (see page 16).
1st row (RS) K7, [p5, k7] 4 times.
2nd row P7, [k5, p7] 4 times.
3rd row K7, [p2tog, p1, p2tog, k7] 4 times. 47 sts.
4th row P7, [k3, p7] 4 times.
5th row Ssk, k3, k2tog, [p3, ssk, k3, k2tog] 4 times. 37 sts.
6th row P5, [k3, p5] 4 times.
7th row K5, [p3tog, k5] 4 times. 29 sts.
8th row P5, [k1, p5] 4 times.
9th row Ssk, k1, k2tog, [p1, ssk, k1, k2tog] 4 times. 19 sts.
10th and 12th rows P3, [k1, p3] 4 times.
11th row K3, [p1, k3] 4 times.
13th row S2kpo, [p1, s2kpo] 4 times. 9 sts.
14th and 16th rows P1, [k1, p1] 4 times.
15th row K1, [p1, k1] 4 times.
17th row Sk2po, p1, k1, p1, k2tog, slip st just made on to left-hand needle, pass next st over it, slip it back on to right-hand needle. 5 sts.
18th row P1, [k1, p1] twice.
19th row K1, s2kpo, k1. 3 sts.
20th row P3.
21st row S2kpo. Slip remaining one st on to left-hand needle and make a 6-st chain (see page 17). Press lightly.

12 SCALLOP SHELL

directory view page 35

Yarn DK yarn in pink (A) and pale pink (B)
Needles 2 pairs of knitting needles, one a size smaller than the other

METHOD

Note The shell is worked from the top.

Using larger-size needles and A, cast on 5 sts by knitted cast-on method (see page 16).
1st row (RS) K.
2nd row P.
3rd row Cast on 3 sts, p3, k5. 8 sts.
4th row Cast on 3 sts, k3, p5, k3. 11 sts.
5th row Cast on 5 sts, [k5, p3] twice. 16 sts.
6th row Cast on 5 sts, p5, [k3, p5] twice. 21 sts.
7th row Cast on 3 sts, [p3, k5] 3 times. 24 sts.
8th row Cast on 3 sts, k3, [p5, k3] 3 times. 27 sts.
9th row Cast on 3 sts, k3, [p3, k5] 3 times, p3. 30 sts.
10th row Cast on 3 sts, p3, [k3, p5] 3 times, k3, p3. 33 sts.
11th row K3, p3, ssk, k1, k2tog, p3, k5, p3, ssk, k1, k2tog, p3, k3. 29 sts.
12th row [P3, k3] twice, p5, [k3, p3] twice.
13th row [K3, p3] twice, ssk, k1, k2tog, [p3, k3] twice. 27 sts.
14th row P3, [k3, p3] 4 times.
15th row Change to B, k3, [p3, k3] 4 times.
16th row As 14th row.
17th row K3, p3tog, [k3, p3tog] 3 times, k3. 19 sts.
18th row Change to A, p3, [k1, p3] 4 times.
19th row K3, [p1, k3] 4 times.
20th row Change to B, work as 18th row.
21st row S2kpo, [p1, s2kpo] 4 times. 9 sts.
22nd row P1, [k1, p1] 4 times.
23rd row K1, [p1, k1] 4 times.
24th row As 22nd row.
25th row S2kpo, p1, k1, p1, k2tog, slip st just made on to left-hand needle, pass next st over it, slip it back on to right-hand needle. 5 sts.
26th row P1, [k1, p1] twice.
27th row K1, s2kpo, k1. 3 sts.
28th row P.
29th row S2kpo. Fasten off remaining one st.

WINGS Using A and smaller-size needles, RS facing and starting at 28th, pick up and k7 sts along B row-ends of right-hand edge.
1st, 3rd, and 5th rows (WS) K.
2nd row Ssk, k3, k2tog. 5 sts.
4th row Ssk, k1, k2tog. 3 sts.
6th row Sk2po. Fasten off remaining one st.
Work left-hand edge to match.
TOP EDGE Using smaller-size needles and A, with RS facing and working into each cast-on st, pick up and k36 sts around top edge, taking 1 st from each st plus 1 extra st from cast-on of each 5-st rib.
Next row Using-larger size needles, k4, kfb, [k8, kfb] 3 times, k4. 40 sts. Bind off knitwise.
Press to shape.

13 STARFISH
directory view page 34

Yarn DK yarn

METHOD

Cast on 4 sts by knitted cast-on method (see page 16).
1st row (RS) [Kfb] 4 times. 8 sts.
2nd row K.
3rd row K1, [m1, k1] 7 times. 15 sts.
4th row K.
5th row K1, m1, [k3, m1] 4 times, k2. 20 sts.
6th row K.
7th row K1, m1, [k2, m1] 9 times, k1. 30 sts.
8th row K.
** **9th row** (RS) K3, m1, k3, turn. Continue on these 7 sts.
10th, 11th, and 12th rows K.
13th row K2, sk2po, k2. 5 sts.
14th, 15th, and 16th rows K.
17th row K1, sk2po, k1. 3 sts.
18th, 19th, and 20th rows K.
21st row Sk2po. One st.
22nd row K. Fasten off.
Rejoining yarn each time, repeat from ** 4 times more.
FINISHING Do not press. Gather cast-on edge, then seam
first 8 rows. Lightly press seam.

14 SPRAT
directory view page 34

Yarn 4-ply-weight metallic yarn used double
Needles 2 pairs of knitting needles, one a size smaller than the other
Extras Batting, flat matt silver sequins and 2 larger faceted silver
sequins, transparent sewing thread

METHOD

Using larger needles, cast on 3 sts.
1st and WS rows P.
2nd row K1, [m1, k1] twice. 5 sts.
4th row K1, [m1, k1] 4 times. 9 sts.
6th row [K1, m1] 3 times, k3, [m1, k1] 3 times. 15 sts.
Beginning with a p row, work 3 rows st-st.
10th row [K3, m1] twice, k3, [m1, k3] twice. 19 sts.
Work 7 rows st-st.
18th row K3, skpo, k2tog, k5, skpo, k2tog, k3. 15 sts.
Work 5 rows st-st.
24th row K2, skpo, k2tog, k3, skpo, k2tog, k2. 11 sts.
Work 3 rows st-st.
28th row K1, skpo, k2tog, k1, skpo, k2tog, k1. 7 sts.
Change to smaller-size needles. Work 3 rows st-st.
32nd row Skpo, k1, [m1, k1] twice, k2tog. 7 sts.
33rd and 35th rows P1, [k1, p1] 3 times.
34th row K1, [p1, k1] 3 times.
36th row K1, [pfb, k1] 3 times. 10 sts. Bind off knitwise.
FINISHING Taking in half a st from each edge, join back
seam with ladder st (see page 21), lightly filling with batting
and finishing at decreases of 32nd row to leave tail free.
Starting 1in (2.5cm) from the tail end, sew overlapping
flat matt silver sequins on the body. For each eye, sew a
smaller flat sequin over a larger, faceted one.

15 CHRISTMAS ROSE

directory view page 43

Yarn DK yarn in white (A), DK cotton in pale green (B), and yellow (C)
Extra A spare needle

METHOD

Note The petals are worked from the top.

PETALS (make 5)
Using A, cast on 5 sts by the thumb method (see page 16).
1st row (RS) Kfb, k2, kfb, k1. 7 sts.
2nd and WS rows P.
3rd row K1, m1, k5, m1, k1. 9 sts.
5th row K1, m1, k7, m1, k1. 11 sts.
7th, 9th, and 11th rows K.
13th row K1, ssk, k5, k2tog, k1. 9 sts.
15th row K1, ssk, k3, k2tog, k1. 7 sts.
17th row K1, ssk, k1, k2tog, k1. 5 sts. Leave sts on a spare needle.
When 5 petals have been completed, slip them all on to one needle, WS facing, and bind off all 25 sts knitwise. Join both ends of the bind-off to make a ring.
CENTER Using B, cast on 4 sts.
1st row K.
2nd row P3, k1. Repeat 1st and 2nd rows 9 times more. Change to C.
STAMENS 1st row K.
2nd row P3, k1.
3rd row Cast on 5 sts by knitted cast-on method (see page 16), bind off 5 sts knitwise, k to end.
4th row P3, k1. Repeat these 4 rows 14 times more, or until, coiled, the strip fits the ring of petals. Bind off.
FINISHING Starting at cast-on edge of center, coil the stamen strip, reverse st-st to the outside, stitch it through the base and catch it down just below the stamens. Set the coil in the center of the petals, turn upside-down and backstitch the bound-off edge of the petals around the base of the coil. Catch the last few rows of each petal to the next and catch these to the coil just below the stamens. Press the petals very lightly.

16 MISTLETOE

directory view page 42

Yarn DK yarn
Extras 2 double-pointed needles, 2 pearlized buttons or beads

METHOD

Note If you prefer knitted berries make them as the holly berries (see page 58).

Using a pair of needles, cast on 5 sts by the thumb method (see page 16).
1st row (RS) Kfb, k2, kfb, k1. 7 sts.
2nd and WS rows K.
3rd row Kfb, k4, kfb, k1. 9 sts.
5th and 7th rows K.
9th row K1, k2tog, k6. 8 sts.
11th row K1, k2tog, k5. 7 sts.
13th row K1, k2tog, k4. 6 sts.
15th row K.
17th row K1, k2tog, k3. 5 sts.
19th row K.
21st row K1, k2tog, k2. 4 sts.
23rd row K.
25th row K1, k2tog, k1. 3 sts.
27th row K.
29th row Kfb, k2. 4 sts.
31st row K.
33rd row Kfb, k3. 5 sts.
35th row K.
37th row Kfb, k4. 6 sts.
39th row Kfb, k5. 7 sts.
41st row Kfb, k6. 8 sts.
43rd row Kfb, k7. 9 sts.
45th and 47th rows K.
49th row K1, k2tog, k3, k2tog, k1. 7 sts.
51st row K1, k2tog, k1, k2tog, k1. 5 sts. Bind off knitwise.
STEM Using double-pointed needles, cast on 2 sts. Make a 2in (5cm) long cord (see page 17). Bind off.
FINISHING Curving the lower edge, press to shape. Attach stem and sew on berries.

17   HOLLY LEAF AND BERRIES
directory view page 42

Yarn Tapestry yarn in dark green (A) and scarlet (B)
Needles 2 pairs of knitting needles, one a size smaller than the other, 2 double-pointed needles

METHOD

LEAF
FIRST SECTION Using larger size needles and A, cast on 20 sts by knitted cast-on method (see page 16).
1st row (RS) K2tog, k16, ssk. 18 sts.
2nd and WS rows K.
3rd row K2tog, k14, ssk. 16 sts.
5th row K2tog, k12, ssk. 14 sts.
7th row K2tog, k10, ssk. 12 sts.
9th row K2tog, k8, ssk. 10 sts. **
10th row K. Break yarn but leave sts on the needle. Using smaller-size needle, RS facing, pick up and k9 sts along first shaped edge, k10 sts from needle, pick up and k9 sts along 2nd shaped edge. 28 sts. Change to larger needles.
Next row [Cast on 3 sts, bind off 7 sts] 5 times, bind off remaining 7 sts. Fasten off.
SECOND SECTION Work as first section to **, so ending with a RS row. Break yarn but leave sts on the needle. Using smaller-size needle, WS facing, pick up and k8 sts along first shaped edge, k10 sts from needle, pick up and k8 sts along 2nd shaped edge. 26 sts. Change to larger needles.
Next row Kfb, k23, kfb, k1. 28 sts.
Next row Bind off 4 sts, [cast on 3 sts, bind off 7 sts] 4 times, bind off remaining 7 sts. Fasten off.

FINISHING Place the 2 sections RS together and, starting at the top of the leaf, using smaller-size needles, * pick up and k1 in first pair of cast-on sts; repeat from * in next pair of sts, then bind off first st. Continue to bind off both cast-on edges together in this way, then the row ends of the picot edge. Using double-pointed needles, (k1, yo, k1) in remaining st. Make a 3-st cord 1⅛in (3cm) long (see page 17). Fasten off. Secure base of stem. Press picot edges only.

BERRY Using B, cast on 2 sts.
1st row (RS) (Kfb, k1) in first st, kfb in 2nd st. 5 sts.
2nd and 4th rows P.
3rd row K.
5th row Ssk, k1, k2tog. 3 sts. Break yarn and draw through sts. Use this end to gather and stitch all edges, while padding the berry with the first end.

18 ELDER LEAF
directory view page 26

Yarn DK yarn

METHOD

STEM Make a 30-st chain (see page 17), ending with one st on left-hand needle.

TOP LEAF (make one)

** **1st row** (RS) (K1, [yo, k1] 4 times) in this one st. 9 sts.

2nd, 3rd, and 4th rows K.

5th row K2tog, k5, skpo. 7 sts.

6th, 8th, and 10th rows K.

7th row K2tog, k3, skpo. 5 sts.

9th row K2tog, k1, skpo. 3 sts.

11th row K.

12th row K3tog. Fasten off remaining one st.

SIDE LEAVES (make 4) Make a 4-st chain, ending with one st on left-hand needle. Work as top leaf from **. Press, then attach shorter stems to main stem.

19 MAPLE LEAF
directory view page 29

Yarn DK yarn
Extra 2 double-pointed needles

METHOD

Note Slip all center slip sts purlwise.

Cast on 11 sts.

1st row (RS) K2, yo, k3, slip 1, k3, yo, k2. 13 sts.

2nd and WS rows K to center st, p1, k to end.

3rd row K2, yo, k4, slip 1, k4, yo, k2. 15 sts.

5th row K2, yo, k5, slip 1, k5, yo, k2. 17 sts.

7th row K2, yo, k6, slip 1, k6, yo, k2. 19 sts.

9th row K2, yo, k7, slip 1, k7, yo, k2. 21 sts.

11th row K2, yo, k8, slip 1, k8, yo, k2. 23 sts.

13th row Cast off 6 sts knitwise, k5 (including st already on needle), slip 1, k11. 17 sts.

14th row Cast off 6 sts, k5, p1, k5. 11 sts.

15th row As 1st row. 13 sts.

17th row As 3rd row. 15 sts.

19th row As 5th row. 17 sts.

21st row As 7th row. 19 sts.

23rd row Bind off 4 sts, k5, slip 1, k9. 15 sts.

24th row Bind off 4 sts, k5, p1, k5. 11 sts.

25th row K3, ssk, slip 1, k2tog, k3. 9 sts.

26th and WS rows As 2nd row.

27th row K2, ssk, slip 1, k2tog, k2. 7 sts.

29th row K1, ssk, slip 1, k2tog, k1. 5 sts.

31st row Ssk, slip 1, k2tog. 3 sts.

33rd row S2kpo. Fasten off remaining one st.

STALK Using double-pointed needles, make a 3-st cord 1⅜in (3.5cm) long (see page 17).

FINISHING Press to shape and attach stalk to WS of leaf.

20 ELM LEAF
directory view page 28

Yarn 4-ply yarn
Extra 2 double-pointed needles

METHOD

Note Slip all center slip sts purlwise with yarn at back.
The leaf is worked from the top.

Cast on 9 sts.
1st row (RS) [K1, yo] twice, ssk, slip 1, k2tog, [yo, k1] twice.
11 sts.
2nd and WS rows K1, p to last st, k1.
3rd row [K1, yo] twice, k1, ssk, slip 1, k2tog, k1, [yo, k1] twice. 13 sts.
5th row [K1, yo] twice, k2, ssk, slip 1, k2tog, k2, [yo, k1] twice. 15 sts.
7th row [K1, yo] twice, k3, ssk, slip 1, k2tog, k3, [yo, k1] twice. 17 sts.
9th row [K1, yo] twice, k4, ssk, slip 1, k2tog, k4, [yo, k1] twice. 19 sts.
11th row K6, sk2po, slip 1, k2sso, k6. 15 sts.
13th row K4, sk2po, slip 1, k2sso, k4. 11 sts.
15th row K2, sk2po, slip 1, k2sso, k2. 7 sts.
17th row Sk2po, slip 1, k2sso. 3 sts.
18th row P3.
Slip these 3 sts on to a double-pointed needle and make a
1in (2.5cm) cord (see page 17).

Specific abbreviation **k2sso** k2tog, slip the st just made
on to the left-hand needle, pass the next st over it, then
return the st to the right-hand needle.

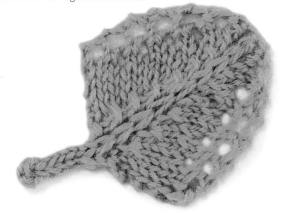

21 BEECH LEAF
directory view page 28

Yarn DK yarn

METHOD

STEM Make an 8-st chain (see page 17),
ending with a st on left-hand needle.
LEAF 1st row (RS) (K1, yo, k1) in this one st.
3 sts.
2nd row P.
3rd row K1, [yo, k1] twice. 5 sts.
4th row P1, [k1, p1] twice.
5th row K1, p1, yo, k1, yo, p1, k1. 7 sts.
6th row P1, k1, p3, k1, p1.
7th row K1, p1, k1, yo, k1, yo, k1, p1, k1. 9 sts.
8th row P1, [k1, p1] 4 times.
9th row [K1, p1] twice, yo, k1, yo,
[p1, k1] twice. 11 sts.
10th row [P1, k1] twice, p3, [k1, p1] twice.
11th row [K1, p1] twice, k1, yo, k1, yo, k1,
[p1, k1] twice. 13 sts.
12th row P1, [k1, p1] 6 times.
13th and 14th rows Rib as set on these and
WS rows.
15th row Skpo, rib 9, k2tog. 11 sts.
17th row Skpo, rib 7, k2tog. 9 sts.
19th row Skpo, rib 5, k2tog. 7 sts.
21st row Skpo, rib 3, k2tog. 5 sts.
23rd row Skpo, k1, k2tog. 3 sts.
25th row S2kpo. Fasten off.

22 WHITEBEAM LEAF
directory view page 28

Yarn DK yarn

METHOD

STEM Make a 10-st chain (see page 17), ending with a st on left-hand needle.
LEAF 1st row (RS) (K1, yo, k1) in this one st. 3 sts.
2nd row P3.
3rd row K1, m1R, k1, m1L, k1. 5 sts.
4th and WS rows K first and last sts, p sts between.
5th row K2, m1R, k1, m1L, k2. 7 sts.
7th row K3, m1R, k1, m1L, k3. 9 sts.
9th row K4, m1R, k1, m1L, k4. 11 sts.
11th row K5, m1R, k1, m1L, k5. 13 sts.
13th and 15th rows K.
17th row K5, s2kpo, k5. 11 sts.
19th row K4, s2kpo, k4. 9 sts.
21st row K3, s2kpo, k3. 7 sts.
23rd row K2, s2kpo, k2. 5 sts.
24th and 26th rows P.
25th row K1, s2kpo, k1. 3 sts.
27th row S2kpo. Fasten off remaining one st.
WS facing, pin to shape and press.

23 POPLAR LEAF
directory view page 28

Yarn DK yarn

METHOD

Note Slip all centre slip sts purlwise with yarn at back.

STEM Cast on 10 sts by thumb method (see page 16), bind off 9 sts knitwise, do not turn, drop left-hand needle to leave one st on right-hand needle.
LEAF 1st row (WS) Yo, k1b in nearest st of cast-on row. 3 sts. Turn and resume with 2 needles.
2nd row K1, p1, k1.
3rd row K1, m1, slip 1, m1, k1. 5 sts.
4th and RS rows K all sts except center st, p this st.
5th row K2, m1, slip 1, m1, k2. 7 sts.
7th row K3, m1, slip1, m1, k3. 9 sts.
9th row K4, m1, slip 1, m1, k4. 11 sts.
11th row K5, m1, slip 1, m1, k5. 13 sts.
13th and 15th rows K.
17th row K5, s2kpo, k5. 11 sts.
19th row K4, s2kpo, k4. 9 sts.
21st row K3, s2kpo, k3. 7 sts.
23rd row K2, s2kpo, k2. 5 sts.
25th row K1, s2kpo, k1. 3 sts.
27th row S2kpo. Fasten off remaining one st.
WS facing, pin to shape and press.

24 LOGANBERRY LEAF
directory view page 36

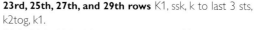

Yarn DK yarn
Needles 2 double-pointed needles

METHOD

SMALL LEAF (make 2)
Using double-pointed needles, cast on 3 sts and make a
⅝in (1.5cm) length of cord (see page 17). Do not bind off,
turn and work k1, p1, k1.
Change to pair of needles.
1st row (RS) K1, m1, k1, m1, k1. 5 sts.
2nd, 4th, 6th, 8th, 10th, and 12th rows K to center st, p1,
k to end.
3rd row K2, m1, k1, m1, k2. 7 sts.
5th row K3, m1, k1, m1, k3. 9 sts.
7th row K4, m1, k1, m1, k4. 11 sts.
9th row K5, m1, k1, m1, k5. 13 sts.
11th row K6, m1, k1, m1, k6. 15 sts.
13th–18th rows K.
19th row K1, ssk, k to last 3 sts, k2tog, k1. 13 sts.
20th, 21st, and 22nd rows K.

23rd, 25th, 27th, and 29th rows K1, ssk, k to last 3 sts,
k2tog, k1.
24th, 26th, 28th, 30th, and 32nd rows K.
31st row K1, sk2po, k1. 3 sts.
33rd row Sk2po. Fasten off remaining one st.
LARGE LEAF (make 1)
Using double-pointed needles, cast on 3 sts and make a
1¾in (4.5cm) length of cord (see page 17). Do not bind
off, turn and work k1, p1, k1. 3 sts.
Change to pair of needles.
1st row (RS) K1, m1, k1, m1, k1. 5 sts.
2nd, 4th, 6th, 8th, 10th, 12th, and 14th rows K to center
st, p1, k to end of row.
3rd row K2, m1, k1, m1, k2. 7 sts.
5th row K3, m1, k1, m1, k3. 9 sts.
7th row K4, m1, k1, m1, k4. 11 sts.
9th row K5, m1, k1, m1, k5. 13 sts.
11th row K6, m1, k1, m1, k6. 15 sts.
13th row K7, m1, k1, m1, k7. 17 sts.
15th–24th rows K.
25th row K1, ssk, k to last 3 sts, k2tog, k1. 15 sts.
26th, 27th, and 28th rows K.
29th, 31st, 33rd, 35th, and 37th rows K1, ssk, k to last
3 sts, k2tog, k1.
30th, 32nd, 34th, 36th, 38th, and 40th rows K.
39th row K1, sk2po, k1. 3 sts.
41st row Sk2po. Fasten off remaining one st.
FINISHING Arrange stalks of pair of small leaves at
an angle about halfway down stalk of large leaf and
sew in place.

Specific abbreviation **m1** make a stitch by lifting strand in
front of next st and knit in front of it.

25 LOGANBERRY
directory view page 36

Yarn DK yarn in crimson (A) and green (B)
Extras Batting, 72 silver-lined red glass beads with holes large enough to take yarn, plus a few extra

METHOD

Note Use needles smaller than usual for the yarn weight to make a firm fabric. Thread beads on to yarn before casting on.

BERRY (make one back and one front)
Using A, cast on 3 sts.
1st row (WS) Kfb, p1, kfb. 5 sts.
2nd row [K1, b1] twice, k1.
3rd row Kfb, p3, kfb. 7 sts.
4th, 6th, and 8th rows [K1, b1] to last st, k1.
5th row Kfb, p5, kfb. 9 sts.
7th row Kfb, p7, kfb. 11 sts.
9th, 11th, 13th, 15th, and 17th rows K1, p9, k1.
10th and 14th rows K2, [b1, k1] to last st, k1.
12th and 16th rows [K1, b1] to last st, k1.
18th row Ssk, [b1, k1] to last 3 sts, b1, k2tog. 9 sts.
19th row K1, p7, k1. Bind off.
CALYX Using B, cast on 8 sts.
1st row (WS) Bind off 5 sts, k2. 3 sts.
2nd row K3, turn, cast on 5 sts. 8 sts.
Repeat 1st and 2nd rows 4 times. Bind off.
FINISHING Sew back and front together, but not joining bound-off edges at top. Stuff firmly, then join bound-off edges. Add a few beads to seams. RS on outside, roll calyx and secure bound-off edge, then sew to top of loganberry.

Specific abbreviation **b1** bring yarn to front, slip next stitch purlwise, slide bead along yarn so that it sits snugly against work, take yarn to back ready to knit next stitch.

26 LEMON SLICE
directory view page 37

Yarn DK yarn in lemon (A) and cream (B)
Extra Crochet hook, spare yarn in contrasting color

METHOD

Note Slip stitches knitwise with yarn at back of work. Do not break off yarn at each color change, but carry yarn not in use up side of work.

Using crochet hook and spare yarn, make 12ch. Fasten off. Using A, pick up and k10 sts in the back loops of the chain and k1 row.
* Continue with A.
1st row K.
2nd row Slip 1, k3, turn, k to end.
3rd row Slip 1, k5, turn, k to end.
4th row Slip 1, k7, turn, k to end.
5th row Slip 1, k5, turn, k to end.
6th row Slip 1, k3, turn, k to end.
7th row Slip 1, k to end. ** Continue with B.
8th row (RS) K.
9th row Slip 1, k to end.
Repeat from * 3 times more, then from * to ** once again.
Break off A.
With RS facing, using crochet hook and B, work across sts on needle in crochet, working 1sc in each st as you slip it off the needle, 2sc in corner, 1sc in each garter ridge around large curve, 2sc in corner. Remove starting chain, slipping each st carefully on to knitting needle and work 1sc in each st. Continuing across small curve, work 1sc, 1hdc, [2-st tr decrease] twice, 1hdc, 1sc in curve. Join by stitching loop to first sc. Fasten off.
With RS facing and large curve at top, rejoin B in right-hand corner of curve. Work 1sc in each sc along large curve, working 2sc in each sc where A wedges meet.
With RS facing and large curve at top, join A in first sc of last row.
Work 1sc in back loop of each sc along large curve. Fasten off.

27 SMOOTH CATERPILLAR

directory view page 37

Yarn 4-ply yarn in green (A) and lime green (B)
Needles 2 pairs, one pair a size smaller than the other
Extra 2 sequins

METHOD

Using larger needles and A, cast on 5 sts.
1st row (RS) Pfb, p2, pfb, p1. 7 sts.
2nd and 4th rows K.
3rd row Pfb, p4, pfb, p1. 9 sts.
5th row K.
6th row P.
7th row P.
8th row K.
9th row P.
10th row K. Repeat 5th–10th rows 3 times more, then work 5th and 6th rows again.
31st row P1, p2tog, p3, p2tog, p1. 7 sts.
32nd row K.
33rd row P1, [p2tog, p1] twice. 5 sts. Bind off knitwise.
LEGS AND UNDERSIDE Using smaller-size needles and B, with RS facing, along one side pick up and k3 sts from shaped edge, [one st from st-st, 3 sts from reverse st-st] 4 times, one st from st-st, 3 sts along remaining shaped edge. 23 sts.
P 1 row. K 1 row.
Next row P1, [yo, p2tog] 11 times.
K 1 row. P 1 row.
Next row [Insert right-hand needle in st on left-hand needle, then in corresponding B loop of pick-up row, k both sts tog] 23 times. Bind off purlwise.
Work 2nd side to match.
FINISHING Seam bound-off edges on underside. Stuff by threading several strands of A on to yarn needle and taking them through body. Neaten each end of caterpillar. Sew on sequins for eyes.

28 STRIPED CATERPILLAR

directory view page 30

Yarn DK cotton in lime green (A) and black (B)
Extras Yellow tapestry wool, batting, 18 black beads, 2 green sequins

METHOD

Using A, cast on 5 sts.
1st row (WS) P.
2nd row [Kfb] 5 times. 10 sts.
3rd row P.
4th row K2, [m1, k1] 8 times. 18 sts.
5th row P.
6th and 7th rows Using B, st-st 2 rows.
8th–11th rows Using A, st-st 4 rows. Repeat 6th–11th rows 6 times more, then work 6th–9th rows again.
Next row (RS) [K1, k2tog] 6 times. 12 sts. St-st one more row A, 2 rows B, 4 rows A, then thread yarn through sts and draw up for tail.
FINISHING Using yellow tapestry wool, make 3 French knots in the center of each black stripe. Join row ends and fill with batting. Gather cast-on sts to close head. Using B, make a loop to draw up the body in each green section except the head and tail. Stitch a pair of beads on the underside of each B stripe. Add sequins for eyes.

SLUG
directory view page 30

Yarn 4-ply yarn in dark gray (A) and pale gray (B)
Needles 2 pairs, one pair a size small than the other, 2 double-pointed needles in the smaller size
Extras Batting, 2 pins with black heads

METHOD

HORNS (make 2)
Using A and double-pointed needles, cast on 2 sts. Make a 3-row cord (see page 17). Leave sts on a spare needle.
BODY Using larger size needles and A, cast on 3 sts.
1st row (RS) [Kfb] twice, k1. 5 sts.
2nd, 4th, 6th, 8th, and 10th rows P.
3rd row K1, [m1, k1] 4 times. 9 sts.
5th row K4, k2 sts of first horn, bring horn to RS, k1, k2 sts of 2nd horn, bring horn to RS, k4. 13 sts.
7th row K5, m1, k3, m1, k5. 15 sts.
9th row K5, [m1, k5] twice. 17 sts.
11th row K1, [p1, k1] 8 times.
12th row P1, [k1, p1] 8 times.
Repeat 11th and 12th rows 3 times more.
19th row (RS) Ssk, rib to last 2 sts, k2tog. 15 sts.
20th row P1, rib to last st, p1.
21st row K1, rib to last st, k1.
22nd row As 20th row. Repeat 19th–22nd rows 4 times more, then work 19th and 20th rows again. 5 sts.
41st row (RS) K1, s2kpo, k1. 3 sts. Bind off purlwise.

FRILL RS facing, using smaller-size needles and A, starting at center of cast-on edge, pick up and k33 sts along side edge, ending in center of bound-off edge.
Change to B. P1 row.
Next row K1, [m1, k1] 32 times. 65 sts.
P1 row. Bind off knitwise.
Starting at bound-off edge, work 2nd frill to match.
UNDERSIDE Using larger size needles and A, cast on 2 sts.
1st row (RS) Kfb, k1. 3 sts.
2nd and WS rows P.
3rd row K1, [m1, k1] twice. 5 sts.
5th row K1, m1, k3, m1, k1. 7 sts.
7th row K1, m1, k5, m1, k1. 9 sts.
Beginning with a p row, work 13 rows st-st.
21st row Ssk, k to last 2 sts, k2tog. 7 sts. Decrease in this way on every following 8th row twice. 3 sts.
Beginning with a p row, work 3 rows st-st.
41st row S2kpo. Fasten off.
FINISHING Lightly press ribs widthwise. Join ends of frill. Join underside along picked-up edge of frill, filling with batting as you go. Insert a pin in each horn.

30 HONEY-BEE
directory view page 31

Yarn DK cotton in brown (A) and yellow (B)
Extras Batting, pale yellow organza ribbon, hairspray, black plastic from frozen food container, 2 small black beads, thick sewing thread in black

METHOD

Using A, cast on 4 sts.
1st row (RS) K.
2nd row [Pfb] 4 times. 8 sts.
3rd row K.
4th row P1, m1p, p6, m1p, p1. 10 sts.
5th row K1, m1, k8, m1, k1. 12 sts.
6th row P.
7th row K1, m1, k10, m1, k1. 14 sts.
8th and 9th rows Using B, st-st 2 rows.
10th and 11th rows Using A, st-st 2 rows.
12th and 13th rows Using B, st-st 2 rows.
Change to A and st-st 10 rows.
Thread yarn through sts, draw up and fasten off.
FINISHING Starting at drawn up sts (head), join row ends and add batting before completing seam. Bind with A to form neck. Spray ribbon with hairspray to prevent fraying, then cut wings using template. Thread them through body just above neck. Using template, cut legs from plastic and stitch to underside of body. Sew on beads for eyes and add antennae of thick black thread, stiffened with hairspray.

31 BUMBLE-BEE
directory view page 30

Yarn 4-ply-weight brushed yarn in orange (A) and black (B)
Extras Batting, pale gray organza ribbon, hairspray, felt-tipped pen with fine point, black leather thonging, black sewing thread, 3 black beads, 3 bobby pins

METHOD

Using A, cast on 6 sts.
1st row (RS) [Kfb] 6 times. 12 sts.
2nd row [Pfb, p1] 6 times. 18 sts.
3rd row K.
4th row P.
5th and 6th rows Using B, st-st 2 rows.
7th–10th rows Using A, st-st 4 rows.
11th–20th rows Using B, st-st 10 rows.
21st–24th rows Using A, st-st 4 rows. Change to B.
K 1 row.
26th row [P2tog] 9 times. 9 sts. K 1 row, then thread yarn through sts, draw up and fasten off.
FINISHING Gathering cast-on sts, join row ends and fill with batting before completing seam. Pull a loop tight around body to make neck. Spray ribbon with hairspray to prevent fraying. Using the template, cut wings from ribbon and mark veins with felt-tipped pen. Thread them through the body just above the neck. Pull leather thonging through head for antennae. Add whiskers of black thread, stiffened with hairspray. Sew on beads for eyes and mouth. Push bent bobby pins crosswise through body for legs.

32 FLY

directory view page 31

Yarn 4-ply-weight metallic yarn, black and green used together
Extras Batting, pale gray organza ribbon, hairspray, felt-tipped pen with fine point, 2 yellow glass beads, 4 black bobby pins

METHOD

Using 2 strands of yarn, cast on 4 sts.
1st row (RS) [Kfb, k1] twice. 6 sts.
2nd row P
3rd row K1, m1, k to last st, m1, k1. 8 sts.
4th row P.
5th row As 3rd row. 10 sts.
6th row P.
7th row As 3rd row. 12 sts.
8th row P.
9th row [K1, m1, k2, m1] 3 times, k1, m1, k2. 19 sts.
St-st 8 rows.
18th row P1, [p2tog] 8 times, p2. 11 sts. St-st 4 rows, then thread yarn through sts, draw up, and fasten off.
FINISHING Starting at cast-on edge (tail), join row ends and add batting before closing at underside of head. Gather tight bands of yarn around body to define head and tail. Spray ribbon with hairspray to prevent fraying, then cut out wings using template. Mark veins with felt-tipped pen and thread wings through body. Sew on beads for eyes and push bobby pins from front to back through body for legs.

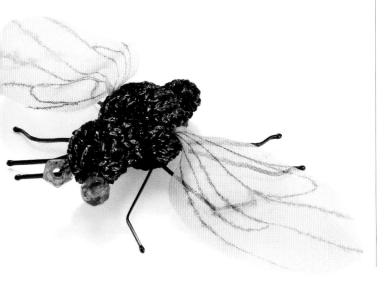

TEMPLATES

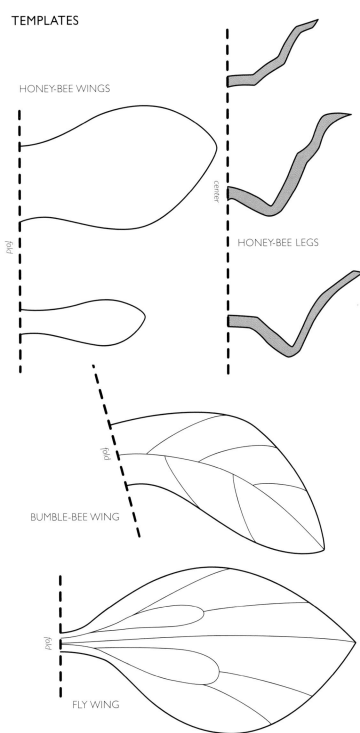

HONEY-BEE WINGS

center

fold

HONEY-BEE LEGS

fold

BUMBLE-BEE WING

fold

FLY WING

33 ACORN

directory view page 40

Yarn DK yarn in olive (A) and beige (B)
Extra Batting

METHOD

ACORN Acorn Using A, cast on 6 sts.
1st row (RS) [Kfb] 6 times. 12 sts.
2nd row [Kfb] 12 times. 24 sts.
3rd row [K1, p1] 12 times.
4th row [P1, k1] 12 times. Repeat 3rd and 4th rows twice more.
9th row [P1, p2tog] 8 times. 16 sts. Continue with B and beginning with a p row, work 7 rows st-st.
17th row [K2tog, k2] 4 times. 12 sts. P one row.
19th row [K2tog, k1] 4 times. 8 sts.
20th row [P2tog] 4 times. Fasten off by running end of yarn through remaining 4 sts.
STEM Using A, cast on 10 sts. Bind off knitwise.
FINISHING Attach stem to cast-on edge of acorn. Join seam with ladder st (see page 21) on RS, filling with batting as you go.

34 FIELD MUSHROOM

directory view page 41

Yarn 4-ply yarn in beige (A) and dark brown (B)

METHOD

Work as Fly Agaric to **.
13th and 14th rows K. Change to B.
15th row K.
16th row [P1, k2] to last st, p1.
Now work as Fly Agaric from *** to **** but adding 2 to each row number. Change to A and work stalk as Fly Agaric, but adding 2 to each row number from 31st to 35th rows.
FINISHING Gather base and, taking in only half a stitch from each edge, join side seam with ladder stitch (see page 21), filling with batting as you go.

35 FLY AGARIC
directory view page 40

Yarn DK yarn in red (A) and white (B). Smaller version in 4-ply, same colors
Extra Batting

METHOD

CAP Using A, cast on 3 sts by the knitted cast-on method (see page 16).
1st row (RS) [K1, yo] twice, k1. 5 sts.
2nd row [P1, p1tbl] twice, p1.
3rd row [K1, yo] 4 times, k1. 9 sts.
4th, 6th, and 8th rows [P1, p1tbl] to last st, p1.
5th row [K1, yo] 8 times, k1. 17 sts.
7th row [K1, yo] 16 times, k1. 33 sts.
9th row [K3, yo] 10 times, k3. 43 sts.
10th row P, working each yo as p1tbl.
11th row K.
12th row P. ** Change to B.
13th and 14th rows K.
*** **15th row** [K1, p2] to last st, k1.
16th row [P1, k2] to last st, p1.
17th row [K1, p2tog] to last st, k1. 29 sts.
18th row [P1, k1] to last st, p1.
19th row [Sk2po, p1] 7 times, k1. 15 sts.
20th row As 18th row.
21st row [Skpo] 7 times, k1. 8 sts. ****
STALK Beginning with a p row, work 9 rows st-st.
31st row [K2, yo] 3 times, k2. 11 sts.
32nd row As 10th row.
33rd row K.
34th row P.
35th row Working k1, [k2tog] 5 times, bind off firmly.
FINISHING Gather base and, taking in only half a stitch from each edge, join side seam with ladder stitch (see page 21), filling with batting as you go. Add spots by splitting B yarn in half and embroidering French knots randomly.

Note In nature this mushroom is poisonous and children should be told not to touch it.

CROCHET DESIGNS

PIGEON FEATHER
directory view page 24

Yarn DK yarn in white (A), gray (B), and charcoal (C)

METHOD

1st row (RS) Using A and leaving an extra long end, make 7ch, miss 3ch, 2dc in next ch. 3 sts.

2nd and 4th rows 1ch, [1sc in next st] to end.

3rd row 4ch, 3tr in next st, 1tr in 1ch. 5 sts.

5th row 5ch, 1dtr in next st, 3dtr in next st, 1dtr in next st, 1dtr in 1ch. 7 sts.

6th row 1ch, 1dc in each st, making last wrap of last dc with B (see page 13).

7th row Using B, 5ch, 1dtr in each of next 2 sts, 3dtr in next st, 1dtr in each of next 3 sts. 9 sts.

8th row 1ch, 1sc in each st, making last wrap of last sc with C.

9th row Using C, 1ch, 1dc in next st, 1tr in each of next 2 sts, 3dtr in next st, 1tr in each of next 2 sts, 1dc in next st, 1sc in 1ch.
Fasten off.

FINISHING Darn in long end behind 3-st ch, then use it to make a few loop sts, anchored with a back st between each. Trim and fray the ends.

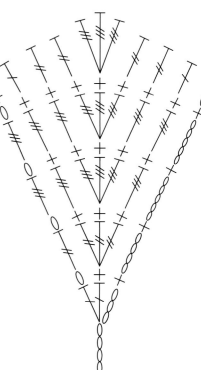

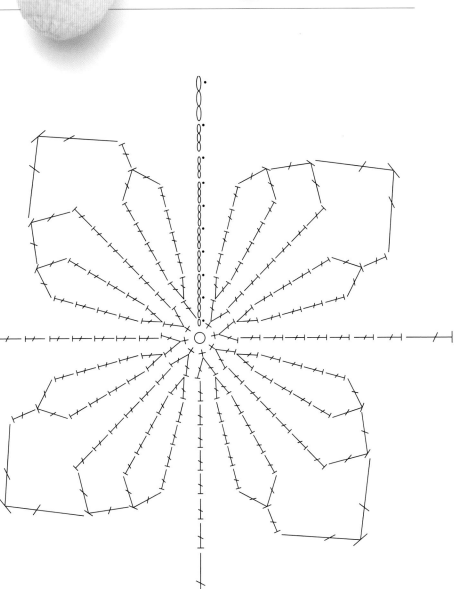

37 HEN'S EGG

directory view page 24

Yarn 4-ply yarn (preferably wool for elasticity)
Extra Egg mold 5in (12.5cm) circumference

METHOD

Make a slip ring (see page 18).
1st round (RS) 2ch, 7sc in ring, pull end to close ring,
ss in top ch of 2ch. 8 sts.
2nd round 3ch, 1tr in ch below, 2dc in each of next 7 sts,
ss in top ch of 3ch. 16 sts.
3rd round 3ch, 2dc in next st, [1dc in next st, 2dc in next st]
7 times, ss in top ch of 3ch. 24 sts.
4th round 3ch, 1dc in each of next 23 sts, ss in top ch
of 3ch.
5th–7th rounds As 4th round.
8th round 3ch, dc dec in next 2 sts, [1dc in next st,
dc dec in next 2 sts] 7 times, ss in top ch of 3ch. 16 sts.
Pull up inside end and fasten off. Insert mold, rounded
end downward.
9th round 3ch, 1dc in next st, dc dec in next 2 sts,
[1dc in each of next 2 sts, dc dec in next 2 sts] 3 times,
ss in top ch of 3ch. 12 sts.
10th round 3ch, dc dec in next 2 sts,
[1dc in next st, dc dec in next 2 sts]
3 times, ss in top ch of 3ch. 8 sts.
Fasten off, leaving a long end. Use this end
to gather sts of last round by taking yarn
under one strand of each st each time.

38 STRAW NEST
directory view page 25

Yarn Natural raffia

METHOD

Note When joining strands it's not necessary to knot them, just leave the ends at the back of the work—this will be the outside.

Make 4ch, join with ss into a ring.

1st round (inside of nest facing) 1ch, 7sc in ring, ss in 1ch. 8 sts.

2nd round 1ch, [2sc in next st, 1sc in next st] 3 times, 2sc in next st, ss in 1ch. 12 sts.

3rd round 1ch, 1sc in next st, [2sc in next st, 1sc in each of next 2 sts] 3 times, 2sc in next st, ss in 1ch. 16 sts.

4th round 1ch, [2sc in next sc, 1sc in next st] 7 times, 2sc in next st, ss in 1ch. 24 sts.

5th round 1ch, 1sc in each of next 2 sts, [2sc in next st, 1sc in each of next 3 sts] 5 times, 2sc in next st, ss in 1ch. 30 sts.

6th round 1ch, 1sc in each of next 3 sts, [2sc in next st, 1sc in each of next 4 sts] 5 times, 2sc in next st, ss in 1ch. 36 sts.

7th round 1ch, 1sc in each st, ss in 1ch.

8th–12th rounds As 7th round.

13th round (In this round before joining new strands, fasten off previous strand with ss.) 1ch, make loop: yarn over middle finger of left hand to make a loop, insert hook in back strand of next st, drop yarn, catch loop and pull it through st and loop on hook as for ss, release loop, pick up yarn, 1sc in back strand of next st; complete round, working random loops and sc, ss in 1ch. Turn.

14th round Work sc, inserting hook in remaining strand of each sc of 12th round (not loop round). Fasten off. Tug base of each loop to tighten, then cut loops, trim and fray ends.

The chart shows 1st–7th rounds. 8th–12th rounds are as 7th round. See instructions for 13th and 14th rounds.

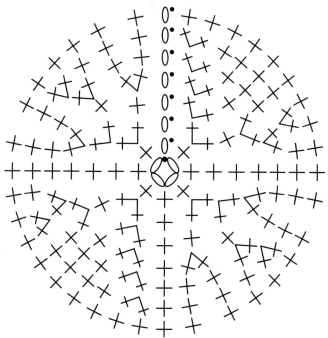

39 FEATHERED NEST

directory view page 25

Yarn DK yarn in light gray
Hooks Two crochet hooks, one a size smaller than the other
Extras Feathers, glue (optional)

METHOD

Note If you find it easier, work with the RS of the sts toward you and invert the nest at the end.

Using larger hook, make 5ch, join with ss into a ring.
1st round (inside of nest) 3ch, 15dc in ring, ss in top ch of 3ch. 16 sts.
2nd round 3ch, 2dc in next st, [1dc in next st, 2dc in next st] 7 times, ss in top ch of 3ch. 24 sts.
3rd round 3ch, 1dc in each of next 2 sts, 2dc in next st, [1dc in each of next 3 sts, 2dc in next st] 5 times, ss in top ch of 3ch. 30 sts.
4th round 3ch, 1dc in each of next 29 sts, ss in top ch of 3ch.
5th round Using smaller hook, make 1ch, 1sc in each of next 29 sts, ss in 1ch. Fasten off.
FINISHING Insert feathers in last round, gluing them in place if necessary.

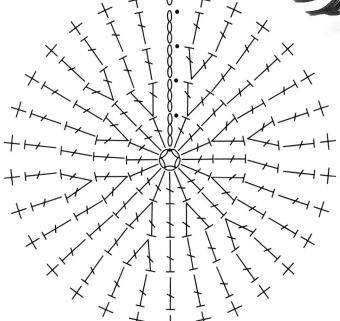

40 LARGE WHITE
directory view page 32

Yarn 4-ply yarn in pale gray (A), white (B), and charcoal gray (C))

METHOD

UPPER RIGHT WING

Using A, make 6ch, join with ss into a ring.

1st row (RS) 3ch, 4dc in ring, making last wrap of 4th dc with B (see page 13) turn. 5 sts.
Continue with B.

2nd row 3ch, 1dc in st below, 1dc in next st, turn and continue on these 3 sts.

3rd row 3ch, 1dc in st below, 1trf in next st, 2dc in top ch of 3ch. 5 sts.

4th row 3ch, 1dc in st below, 1dc in next st, 1trb in next st, 1dc in next st, 2dc in top ch of 3ch. 7 sts.

5th row 3ch, 1trf in next st, [1dc in next st, 1trf in next st] twice, (1dc, 1sc) in top ch of 3ch. 8 sts.

6th row 1ch, 1sc in next st, [1trb in next st, 1dc in next st] twice, 1trb in next st, 1sc in top ch of 3ch. Fasten off.

LOWER RIGHT WING

WS facing, join B in 3rd st of first row.

2nd row 3ch, 2dc in next st, 2dc in top ch of 3ch. 5 sts.

3rd row 3ch, 1dc in st below, 1trf in next st, 1dc in next st, 1trf in next st, 2dc in top ch of 3ch. 7 sts.

4th row 3ch, 1dc in st below, 1dc in next st, [1trb in next st, 1dc in next st] twice, 2dc in top ch of 3ch. 9 sts.

5th row 2ch, 1trf in next st, [1dc in next st, 1trf in next st] 3 times, 1sc in top ch of 3ch.

6th row Ss in each of next 2 sts, 1sc in each of next 3 sts, ss in each of next 2 sts. Fasten off.

Next row RS facing, rejoin A in ring, 3ch, 4dc in ring, making last wrap of 4th dc with B. 5 sts. Turn. Continue with B.

LOWER LEFT WING

2nd row 3ch, 1dc in st below, 2dc in next st, 1dc in next st, turn and continue on these 5 sts.

3rd row 3ch, 1dc in st below, 1trf in next st, 1dc in next st, 1trf in next st, 2dc in top ch of 3ch. 7 sts.

4th row 3ch, 1dc in st below, 1dc in next st, [1trb in next st, 1dc in next st] twice, 2dc in top ch of 3ch. 9 sts.

5th row 2ch, 1trf in next st, [1dc in next st, 1trf in next st] 3 times, 1sc in top ch of 3ch.

6th row Ss in each of next 2 sts, 1sc in each of next 3 sts, ss in each of next 2 sts. Fasten off.

UPPER LEFT WING

WS facing, join B in remaining dc of first row.

2nd row 3ch, 1dc in st below, 1dc in top ch of 3ch. 3 sts.

3rd row 3ch, 1dc in st below, 1trf in next st, 2dc in top ch of 3ch. 5 sts.

4th row 3ch, 1dc in st below, 1dc in next st, 1trb in next st, 1dc in next st, 2dc in top ch of 3ch. 7 sts.

5th row 2ch, 1dc in st below, 1trf in next st, [1dc in next st, 1trf in next st] twice, 1dc in top ch of 3ch. 8 sts.

6th row 2ch, 1trb in next st, [1dc in next dc, 1trb in next st] twice, 1sc in next st, ss in top ch of 2ch. Fasten off.

WING TIPS

Upper right RS facing and using C, join yarn in last tr of 6th row, 1ch, 1sc in each of next 4 sts, 2dc in next st, 1tr in 1ch. Fasten off.

Upper left RS facing and using C, join yarn in ss of 6th row, 4ch, 2dc in next st, 1sc in each of next 4 sts, ss in next st. Fasten off.

BODY

Using C, make 7ch, miss 1ch, ss in each of next 6ch, 3ch, 2dc in last of 7ch, remove hook leaving loop, insert hook in top ch of 3ch then in loop, yrh, pull yarn through. Fasten off.

FINISHING Using C, embroider 2 spots on each upper wing. Sew on body and, using C, make 2 antennae (see page 21). Join each upper and lower wing with a single invisible stitch.

Specific abbreviations **trb** tr made from the back around the stem of the st; **trf** tr made from the front around the stem of the st.

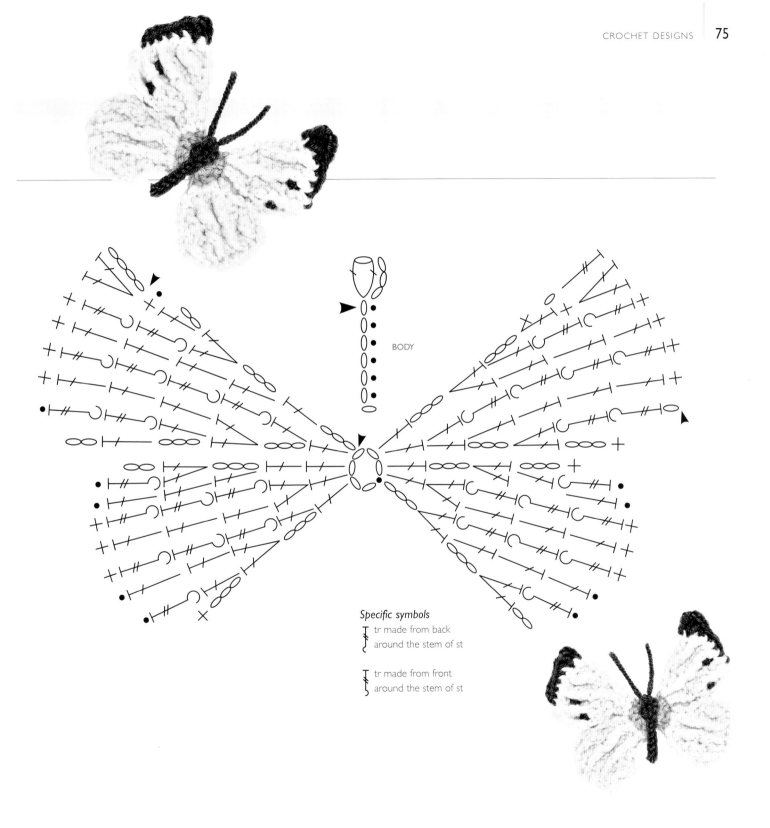

BODY

Specific symbols

tr made from back
around the stem of st

tr made from front
around the stem of st

41 CLOUDED YELLOW
directory view page 32

Yarn 4-ply cotton in yellow (A) and brown (B)
Hooks 2 crochet hooks, one a size smaller than the other

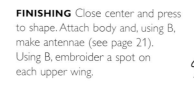

METHOD

RIGHT WINGS
Using larger hook and A, make 9ch, join with ss into a ring.
1st row (RS) 3ch, 7dc in ring, turn. 8 sts.
2nd row 3ch, 1dc in each of next 2 sts, 2dc in each of next 3 sts, 1dc in next st, 1dc in top ch of 3ch. 11 sts.
3rd row 3ch, 1dc in each of next 3 sts, 2tr in next st, 1dc in each of next 2 sts, 2ch, ss in next st, 2ch, 2dc in next st, 2tr in next st, 1tr in top ch of 3ch. 15 sts.
4th row 3ch, 1dc in next st, 2tr in next st, 1dc in next st, 1sc in next st, ss in top ch of 2ch. 6 sts. Fasten off.
5th row Join B in same ch as ss, 3ch, 1dc in each of next 2 sts, 2dc in next st, 1tr in next st, 2-st tr dec in next st and top ch of 3ch. Fasten off.
Next row RS facing, join B in first dc of 3rd row, 1ch, 1sc in each of next 2 sts, 2sc in each of next 3 sts, 1sc in next st, ss in top ch of 2ch.

LEFT WINGS
RS facing, join A in ring.
1st row 3ch, 7dc in ring, turn. 8 sts.
2nd row 3ch, 1dc in next st, 2dc in each of next 3 sts, 1dc in each of next 2 sts, 1dc in top ch of 3ch. 11 sts.
3rd row 4ch, 2tr in next st, 2dc in next st, 2ch, ss in next st, 2ch, 1dc in each of next 2 sts, 2tr in next st, 1dc in each of next 3 sts, 1dc in top ch of 3ch.
Fasten off.
4th row With WS facing, rejoin A in top ch of 2ch of upper wing, 1ch, 1sc in first st, 1dc in next st, 2tr in next st, 1dc in next st, making last wrap with B (see page 13) 1dc in top ch of 4ch. Continue with B.
5th row 3ch, 1tr in each of next 2 sts, 2dc in next st, 1dc in each of next 2 sts, 2ch, ss in 1ch. Fasten off.
Next row RS facing, join B in top ch of 2ch of lower wing, 1ch, 1sc in next st, 2sc in each of next 3 sts, 1sc in each of next 3 sts, ss in last st. Fasten off.

EDGING
Using smaller hook and B, working into one strand of A only, ss along edges of upper and lower wings.

BODY
Using larger hook and B, make 5ch, miss 1ch, ss in each of next 4ch, make 4ch, 3-st tr cluster in top ch of 5ch, 3ch, miss 2ch, 1sc in next ch. Fasten off.

FINISHING Close center and press to shape. Attach body and, using B, make antennae (see page 21). Using B, embroider a spot on each upper wing.

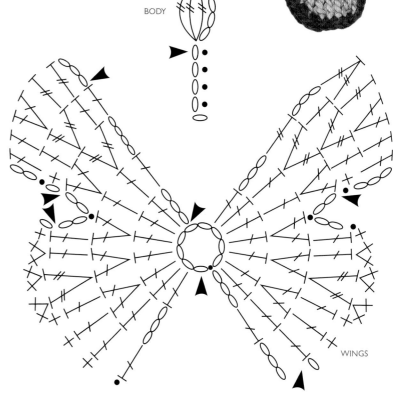

BODY

WINGS

42 BRIMSTONE BUTTERFLY

directory view page 32

Yarn DK yarn in yellow (A), olive green (B), and orange (C)

METHOD

WINGS (made in one row, RS facing)
Using A, make 13ch, miss 5ch, 2dtr in next ch, 5ch, 1sc in 7th of 13ch, 4ch, (1dtr, 1trtr) in 8th of 13ch, 3ch, ss in top of trtr, 6ch, ss in 9th of 13ch, 9ch, miss 2ch, ss in next ch, (1trtr, 1dtr) in 10th of 13ch, 4ch, 1sc in 11th of 13ch, 5ch, 2dtr in 12th of 13ch, 5ch, ss in 13th ch. Fasten off.
BODY (WS) Using B, make 7ch, miss 1ch, 1sc in next ch, ss in each of next 4ch. Fasten off.
FINISHING Gather center, close it and join wings. Press. Stitch body in place. Using C, embroider a spot on each wing. Using B, make antennae (see page 21).

*Specific abbreviation **trtr*** yrh 4 times, insert hook and pull yarn through, [yrh and pull yarn through 2 loops] 5 times.
Specific symbol
As above.

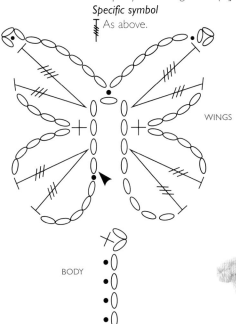

WINGS

BODY

43 GOLDEN HAIRSTREAK

directory view page 32

Yarn Shetland-type 4-ply in ocher (A) and olive (B)

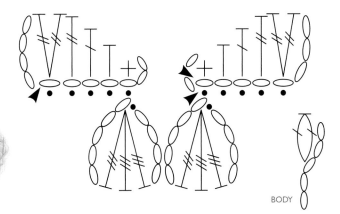

METHOD

FIRST PAIR OF WINGS
UPPER LEFT Using A, make 7ch. Miss 2ch, 1sc in next ch, 1hdc in next ch, 1dc in next ch, 1tr in next ch, 2tr in next ch, 4ch, ss in each remaining strand of the 5ch at the base of the sts.
LOWER LEFT ** 5ch, miss 4ch, 3dtr in next ch, 4ch, ss in same ch as 3dtr. Fasten off. ***
SECOND PAIR OF WINGS
UPPER RIGHT Using A, make 8ch. Miss 3ch, 2tr in next ch, 1tr in next ch, 1dc in next ch, 1hdc in next ch, 1sc in next ch, 2ch, ss in each remaining strand of the 5ch at the base of the sts. Fasten off.
LOWER RIGHT RS facing, rejoin yarn in the ss under the 1sc. Work as lower left wing from ** to ***.
BODY Using B, make 5ch, miss 2ch, in next ch work 2dc without completing last wrap of each, yrh, pull yarn through all 3 loops on hook. Fasten off.
FINISHING Join wings and catch together 2 sts of upper and lower wings invisibly on WS. Press to shape. Turn body over and stitch in place. Using B, make 2 antennae (see page 21).

WINGS

BODY

44 CAMBERWELL BEAUTY
directory view page 32

Yarn DK yarn in dark brown (A), pale yellow (B), and pale blue (C)

METHOD

Using A, make 5ch, join with ss into a ring.
Set-up row (RS) 3ch, 16dc in ring. 17 sts.

RIGHT UPPER WING

1st row 2ch, 1dc in st below, 1dc in each of next 2 sts, 2dc in next st, turn. Continue on these 6 sts.

2nd row 2ch, 1sc in st below, 1sc in each of next 2 sts, 1dc in next st, (1tr; 1dtr) in next st, 1dtr in top ch of 2ch of previous row. 8 sts.

3rd row 3ch, 1dc in st below, 1dc in each of next 2 sts, 1sc in each of next 4 sts, making last wrap with B (see page 13) 1sc in top ch of 2ch. 9 sts. Continue with B.

4th row 2ch, 1sc in st below, 1dc in each of next 4 sts, 2dc in next st, 4ch, miss 3ch, ss in next ch, 2dc in next st, 1dc in next st, 1dc in top ch of 3ch. 12 sts. Fasten off.

LEFT UPPER WING

WS facing, rejoin A in 4th st of set-up row.

1st row 2ch, 1dc in st below, 1dc in each of next 2 sts, 2dc in top ch of 3ch. 6 sts.

2nd row 5ch, (1dtr; 1tr) in next st, 1dc in next st, 1sc in each of next 2 sts, 2sc in top ch of 2ch. 8 sts.

3rd row 2ch, 1sc in each of next 4 sts, 1dc in each of next 2 sts, making last wrap with B, 2dc in top ch of 5ch. 9 sts. Continue with B.

4th row 3ch, 1dc in next st, 2dc in next st, 4ch, miss 3ch, ss in next ch, 2dc in next st, 1dc in each of next 4 sts, 2sc in top ch of 2ch. 12 sts. Fasten off.

RIGHT LOWER WING

WS facing, rejoin A in set-up row in st next to right upper wing.

1st row 3ch, 1dc in st below, 1dc in each of next 2 sts, 2dc in next st. 6 sts.

2nd row 3ch, 1dc in st below, 1dc in next st, 1tr in each of next 2 sts, 1dc in next st, (1dc, 1sc) in top ch of 3ch. 8 sts.

3rd row 2ch, 1sc in each of next 6 sts, making last wrap with B, 2sc in top ch of 3ch. 9 sts. Continue with B.

4th row 1ch, 1sc in each of next 2 sts, 2dc in next st, 4ch, miss 3ch, ss in next ch, 2dc in next st, 1dc in each of next 2sts, 1sc in next st, ss in top ch of 2ch. 11 sts. Fasten off.

LEFT LOWER WING

WS facing, miss st beside right lower wing and rejoin A in next st.

1st row 3ch, 1dc in st below, 1dc in each of next 2 sts, 2dc in next st. 6 sts.

2nd row 2ch, 1dc in st below, 1dc in next st, 1tr in each of next 2 sts, 1dc in next st, 2dc in top ch of 3ch. 8 sts.

3rd row 2ch, 1sc in st below, 1sc in each of next 6 sts, making last wrap with B, 1sc in top ch of 2ch. 9 sts. Continue with B.

4th row 1ch, 1sc in next st, 1dc in each of next 2 sts, 2dc in next st, 4ch, miss 3ch, ss in next ch, 2dc in next st, 1sc in each of next 2 sts, ss in top ch of 2ch. 11 sts. Fasten off.

BODY

Using A, make 6ch, miss 2ch, 1sc in each of 4ch, make 4ch, miss 4ch, 4tr in last sc. Leaving the loop remove hook and insert it first in top ch of 4ch then in loop, yrh, pull yarn through, 3ch, miss 2ch, 1sc in next ch. Fasten off.

FINISHING Stretching widthwise, press to shape. Using C, stitch spots on alternate sts of 3rd row of each wing. Attach body and, using A, make antennae (see page 21). Stitch ends of antennae with C.

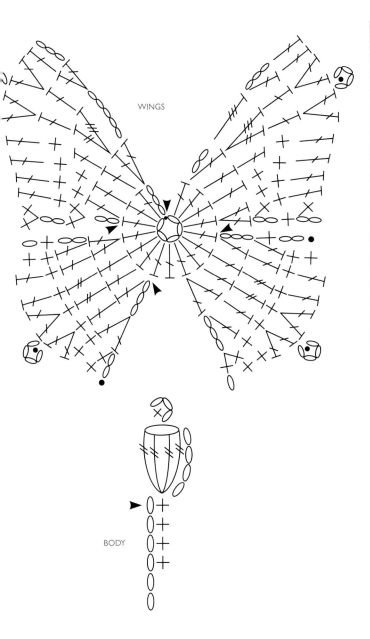

WINGS

BODY

45 | **PEBBLES**
directory view page 34

Yarn DK yarn in light gray, mid gray, and dark gray
Extras Pebbles (choose ones that are smooth and fairly flat; wash and allow to dry before covering)

METHOD

Make 3ch and join with ss into a ring.
6sc in ring and join with ss. Work sc continuously (do not join rounds), marking the first st of every round (see page 20). Increase and decrease as required following the contours of the pebble and aim for a snug fit. Try the cover on the pebble as you work to check the fit. Work all increases as 2sc in one st and decreases as sc dec over next 2 sts (see page 13).
To introduce stripes, change color at the stitch before the marker—work the first part of the sc (insert hook, yrh, pull yarn through) then pull new color through 2 loops on hook to finish the stitch. Work 1 or 2 rounds in the new color, then change yarn as required.
When the cover starts to narrow at the opposite end of the pebble, finish off any yarn ends securely on the wrong side, slip the pebble inside the cover and work the remaining rounds with it in place. Fasten off. Use the yarn end to secure the last few stitches of the cover.

46 SARDINE

directory view page 35

Yarn 4-ply-weight metallic yarn
Extra 2 sequins

METHOD

HEAD AND BODY

Make a slip ring (see page 18).
1st row (RS) 5ch, 10dtr in ring, pull end tightly to close ring, turn. 11 sts.
2nd row 2ch, 1sc in each of next 3 sts, 2sc in next st, 1sc in next st, 2sc in next st, 1sc in each of next 3 sts, 1sc in top ch of 5ch. 13 sts.
3rd row 2ch, working in the back strand of each sc, 1sc in each of next 11 sts, 1sc in top ch of 2ch. Resume working in both strands of each st from here on.
4th row 2ch, 1sc in each of next 4 sts, 2sc in next st, 1sc in next st, 2sc in next st, 1sc in each of next 4 sts, 1sc in top ch of 2ch. 15 sts.
5th row 2ch, 1sc in each st, 1sc in top ch of 2ch.
6th, 7th, 8th, 9th, and 10th rows As 5th row.
11th row 2ch, sc dec in next 2 sts, 1sc in each of next 9 sts, sc dec in next 2 sts, 1sc in top ch of 2ch. 13 sts.
12th, 13th, and 14th rows As 5th row.
15th row 2ch, sc dec in next 2 sts, 1sc in each of next 7 sts, sc dec in next 2 sts, 1sc in top ch of 2ch. 11 sts.
16th, 17th, and 18th rows As 5th row.

19th row 2ch, sc dec in next 2 sts, 1sc in each of next 5 sts, sc dec in next 2 sts, 1sc in top ch of 2ch. 9 sts.
20th row As 5th row.
21st row 2ch, sc dec in next 2 sts, 1sc in each of next 3 sts, sc dec in next 2 sts, 1sc in top ch of 2ch. 7 sts.
22nd row As 5th row.

TAIL

23rd row 5ch, 1tr in st below, 1dc in next st, 2dc in next st, (1tr, 1ch, 1dtr, 1ch, 1tr) in next st, 2dc in next st, 1dc in next st, (1tr, 1dtr) in top ch of 2ch. Fasten off.

FINISHING RS facing and tail downward, join yarn in first st of 2nd row, 1ch, working in single surface strand each time, 1sc in each st to end of row. Fasten off. Join ends of tail and seam, stuffing with spare yarn before completing. Sew on sequins for eyes.

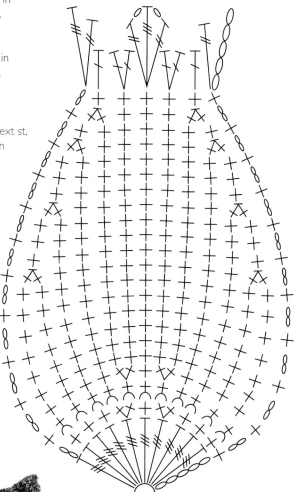

47 GOLDFISH
directory view page 34

Yarn 4-ply yarn
Extras Batting (optional), 2 faceted sequins, and a small quantity of flat sequins

METHOD

BODY
Make a slip ring (see page 18).
1st round (RS) 1ch, 7sc in ring, pull end to close ring, ss in 1ch. 8 sts.
2nd round 1ch, 1sc in each st, ss in 1ch.
3rd round 3ch, 1dc in st below, 1dc in next st, 2dc in next st, 1dc in next st, 3dc in next st, 1dc in next st, 2dc in next st, 1dc in next st, 1dc in ss of round below, ss in top ch of 3ch. 14 sts.
4th round 3ch, 1dc in st below, 1dc in each of next 6 sts, 3dc in next st, 1dc in each of next 6 sts, 1dc in ss of round below, ss in top ch of 3ch. 18 sts.
5th round 3ch, 1dc in st below, 1dc in each of next 8 sts, 3dc in next st, 1dc in each of next 8 sts, 1dc in ss of round below, ss in top ch of 3ch. 22 sts.
6th and 7th rounds 3ch, 1dc in each of next 21 sts, ss in top ch of 3ch.
8th round 3ch, dc dec in next 2 sts, 1dc in each of next 17 sts, 1dc dec in next 2 sts, ss in top ch of 3ch. 20 sts.
9th round 3ch, dc dec in next 2 sts, 1dc in each of next 15 sts, dc dec in next 2 sts, ss in top ch of 3ch. 18 sts.
10th round 3ch, [dc dec in next 2 sts] twice, 1dc in each of next 9 sts, [dc dec in next 2 sts] twice, ss in top ch of 3ch. 14 sts.
11th round 3ch, [dc dec in next 2 sts] twice, 1dc in each of next 5 sts, [dc dec in next 2 sts] twice, ss in top ch of 3ch. 10 sts. Fasten off.

DORSAL FIN
Turn fish so that mouth is to the right. Join yarn around stem of center st of 3-st increase of 5th round.
1st row 1ch, 1sc around this st, 2sc around each center st of 6th, 7th, 8th, and 9th rounds, 1sc around center st of 10th round. 11 sts.

2nd row 2ch, 1dc in each of next 2 sts, 1ch, 1sc in each of next 2 sts, 1ch, 1dc in next st, 2tr in next st, 1tr in each of next 2 sts, tr dec in next st and 1ch. Fasten off.

SMALLER PAIR OF UNDERSIDE FINS
Turn fish so that mouth is to the left.
FIRST FIN
Join yarn in st beside 3ch at start of 5th round. 4ch, 2tr in st below. Fasten off.
SECOND FIN
Turn fish over and join yarn in corresponding st beside 3ch of 4th round. 4ch, 2tr in st below. Fasten off.
LARGER PAIR OF UNDERSIDE FINS
In 8th round, position as smaller pair of fins but work: 5ch, 2dtr in st below. Fasten off.
VENTRAL FIN
1st row With mouth to the left, join yarn in first ch of 3ch at beginning of 10th round: (1ch, 1sc) in this group of 3ch, 2sc in next group. 4 sts.
2nd row Miss 1sc, 1sc in next st, 1dc in next st, 2tr in 1ch. Fasten off.
TAIL
Lightly stuff body with batting or spare yarn. With dorsal fin to the left, flatten tail end, join yarn, and work in both front and back sts together on 1st row.
1st row 1ch in first pair of sts, 1sc in each of next 4 pairs of sts. 5 sts.
2nd row 1ch, 1sc in each of next 4 sts.
3rd row 6ch, miss 2ch, ss in next ch, (1dtr, 1tr, 1dc) in st below, 1dc in each of next 3 sts, (1dc, 1tr, 1dtr) in 1ch. Fasten off.
FINISHING Sew on faceted sequins for eyes. Sew flat sequins on body (see page 21).

48 SEA ANEMONE

directory view page 34

Yarn 4-ply cotton in raspberry (A) and coral (B)

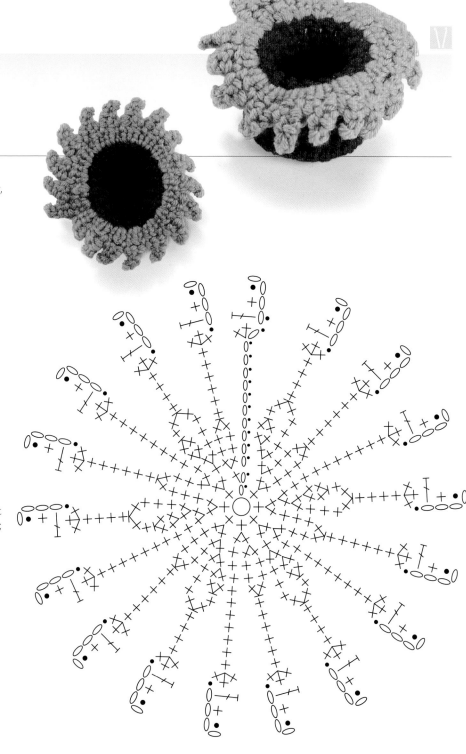

METHOD

Using A, make a slip ring (see page 18).

1st round (RS) 1ch, 7sc in ring, pull end to close ring, ss in 1ch. 8 sts.

2nd round 1ch, 1sc in st below, 2sc in each of next 7 sts, ss in 1ch. 16 sts.

3rd round 1ch, 2sc in next st, [1sc in next st, 2sc in next st] 7 times, ss in 1ch. 24 sts.

4th round 1ch, 1sc in each of next 2 sts, 2sc in next st, [1sc in each of next 3 sts, 2sc in next st] 5 times, ss in 1ch. 30 sts.

5th round 1ch, 1sc in each of next 3 sts, 2sc in next st, [1sc in each of next 4 sts, 2sc in next st] 5 times, ss in 1ch. 36 sts.

6th round 1ch, sc dec in next 2 sts, [1sc in next st, sc dec in next 2 sts] 11 times, ss in 1ch. 24 sts.

7th round 1ch, 1sc in each st, ss in 1ch.

8th round 1ch, 1sc in next st, sc dec in next 2 sts, [1sc in each of next 2 sts, sc dec in next 2 sts] 5 times, ss in 1ch. 18 sts.

9th, 10th, 11th, and 12th rounds As 7th round, working last ss with B. Continue with B.

13th round 1ch, 2sc in st below, 3sc in each of next 17 sts, ss in 1ch. 54 sts.

14th round * 4ch, miss 1ch, ss in next ch, 1sc in next ch, 1dc in next ch, ss in first st of next group of 3 sts; repeat from *, ending ss in first ch of 4ch. Fasten off.

FINISHING Press the points carefully.

49 BRANCHING SEAWEED
directory view page 34

Yarn DK yarn

METHOD

Note Fasten off throughout by pulling yarn through last loop without working yrh.

STEM AND FIRST BRANCH
Make 5ch.

1st row (RS) Miss 2ch, 1dc in each of next 3ch. 4 sts.

2nd and WS rows 2ch, 1dc in each st.

3rd row 2ch, 1dc dec, 1dc in next st. 3 sts.

5th row As 2nd row.

7th row 2ch, 1dc in st below, 2dc in each of next 2 sts. 6 sts.

9th row 2ch, 1dc in st below, 2dc in next st, turn. Continue on these 4 sts.

11th row 2ch, 1dc in st below, 1dc in next st. Continue on these 3 sts.

13th row 2ch, 1dc in st below, 1 popcorn in next st, 2dc in next st. 5 sts.

14th row 1ch, ss in each of next 3 sts. Fasten off.

SECOND BRANCH
1st row (RS) Rejoin yarn in next st of 10th row, 2ch, 2dc in next st. Continue on these 3 sts.

2nd, 3rd, and 4th rows 2ch, 1dc in each of next 2 sts.

5th row 2ch, 1dc in st below, 1 popcorn in next st, 2dc in next st. 5 sts.

6th row 1ch, 1sc in each of next 2 sts, ss in next st. Fasten off.

THIRD BRANCH
1st row (RS) Miss one st of 8th row, rejoin yarn in next st, 2ch, 2dc in each of next 2 sts. 5 sts.

2nd row 2ch, 1dc in each of next 4 sts.

3rd row 2ch, 1dc in st below, 1dc in next st, turn. Continue on these 3 sts.

4th row 2ch, 1dc in each of next 2 sts, turn.

5th row 2ch, 1dc in st below, 1 popcorn in next st, 2dc in next st. 5 sts.

6th row 1ch, 1sc in each of next 2 sts, ss in next st. Fasten off.

FOURTH BRANCH
1st row (RS) In group of 5 sts at base of third branch, miss one st, rejoin yarn in next st, 2ch, 1dc in st below, 2dc in next st. 4 sts.

2nd row 2ch, 1dc in each of next 3 sts.

3rd row 2ch, 1dc in st below, 1dc in next st, turn. Continue on these 3 sts.

4th row 2ch, 1dc in each of next 2 sts.

5th row 2ch, 1dc in st below, 1 popcorn in next st, 2dc in next st. 5 sts.

6th row 1ch, 1sc in each of next 2 sts, ss in next st. Fasten off.

FIFTH BRANCH
1st row (RS) In group of 4 sts at base of fourth branch, rejoin yarn in next st, 2ch, 2dc in next st. 3 sts.

2nd, 3rd, and 4th rows 2ch, 1dc in each of next 2 sts.

5th row 2ch, 1dc in st below, 1 popcorn in next st, 2dc in next st. 5 sts.

6th row 1ch, ss in each of next 3 sts. Fasten off.

FINISHING Press carefully, avoiding popcorns.

Specific stitch **popcorn** 5dc in one st, remove hook, leaving loop, insert hook in top of first dc then in loop, yrh, pull yarn through.

Specific symbol
As above

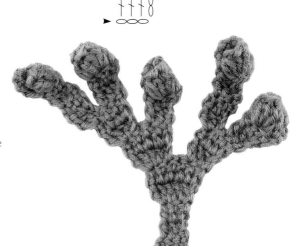

50 EAR OF WHEAT
directory view page 26

Yarn Natural raffia
Extra Fine wire (optional)

METHOD

Make 29ch, miss 3ch, 2dc in next ch, * remove hook leaving loop, insert hook in top ch of 3ch then in loop, yrh, pull yarn through both loops on hook, yrh, pull yarn tightly through remaining loop. Cut yarn, leaving an end of approximately 2in (5cm). ** Miss 1ch, join yarn in next of 29ch (base ch), 3ch, 2dc in base ch, repeat from * to **. Rejoin yarn in remaining strand of same base ch, 3ch, 2dc in same ch, repeat from * to **. Missing 1ch between each pair of clusters, make 4 more pairs in this way.
FINISHING Take a length of fine raffia and ss in each of remaining base ch. Take the first end of each group through the st at the top. Trim and fray the ends. Catch together the groups and wire the stem if necessary.

Specific symbol

3ch, 2dc in ch below, then work as * to ** above.

51 BACHELOR'S BUTTON
directory view page 26

Yarn 4-ply yarn in pink
Extra Small wooden plant stake

METHOD

FLOWER
Make a slip ring (see page 18).
1st round (RS) 2ch, 7sc in ring, pull end to close ring, ss in top ch of 2ch. 8 sts.
2nd round 1ch, working in back strand each time (1sc, 1 petal) in each of 7sc, ss in 1ch. 7 petals.
3rd round Folding back the petals of the previous round to work in front of them and working in both strands of each st (1sc, 1 petal, 1sc, 1 petal) in each sc of previous round, ss in first sc. 14 petals. Fasten off.
4th round Working in front strand of sts of 1st round, join yarn in one sc, 1 picot in this sc, [ss in next sc, 1 picot in this sc] 6 times, ss in base of first picot. Fasten off.
STEM
Insert top of stake in the flower centre.

Specific stitches **petal** 7ch, miss 3ch, ss in each of next 4ch; **picot** 5ch, miss 3ch, ss in each of next 2ch.

1st, 2nd and 3rd rounds

4th round

52 FOXGLOVE

directory view page 26

Yarn 4-ply yarn in pink (A) and green (B)
Extra Strong wire (e.g. fencing wire)

METHOD

LARGER FLOWER (make 7)
Using A, make a slip ring (see page 18).
1st round (RS) 3ch, 5dc in ring, pull end to
close ring, ss in top ch of 3ch.
6 sts. **
2nd round 4ch, 1tr in each of next 5 sts,
ss in top ch of 4ch.
3rd round 3ch, 1dc in st below, 2dc in next
st, 3ch, ss in same st, ss in next st, 4ch, 1tr in
same st, [2tr in next st] twice, 1tr in next st,
4ch, ss in same st. 13 sts. Fasten off.

SMALLER FLOWER (make 5)
Work as larger flower to **.
2nd round 3ch, 1dc in each of next 5dc,
ss in top ch of 3ch.
3rd round 3ch, 2dc in next dc, 3ch, ss in next dc,
1ch, 2sc in in each of next 2dc, ss in next dc.
Fasten off.

CALYX (make 5)
Using B, work as larger flower to **.
2nd round 3ch, 1dc in st below, 1dc in next
st, 3ch, ss in same st, [ss in next st, 3ch, 1dc
in same st, 1dc in next st, 3ch, ss in same st]
twice. 12 sts. Fasten off.

STEM
Bend one end of the wire into a small loop.
Using B, cover the loop and stem with sc,
fastening off securely.

FINISHING Fit each flower into a calyx and
close the ends of the remaining three to
make buds. Starting at the looped end of the
wire, attach the buds, then the smaller flowers,
alternating each one. Attach the larger flowers
in the same way.

CALYX

LARGER
FLOWER

SMALLER
FLOWER

53 SWEET PEA

directory view page 27

Yarn 4-ply yarn in green (A) and pastel colors (B)

METHOD

SEPALS

Using A, make 4ch, join with ss into a ring.

1st round (RS) 4ch, 7tr in ring, RS to the outside, roll into a tube and ss in top ch of 4ch. 8 sts.

2nd round [4ch, miss 3ch, 1sc in next ch, ss in each of next 2 sts] 4 times, ending ss in first ch. 4 sepals. Fasten off.

PETALS

Using B, make 7ch.

1st row (RS) Miss 4ch, 1tr in each of next 3 sts. 4 sts.

2nd row 2ch, 1sc in st below, 2sc in each of next 2 sts, 2sc in top ch of 4ch. 8 sts.

3rd row 2ch, 1hdc in st below, 2dc in next st, 2tr in next st, 2dtr in next st, 1ch, 2dtr in next st, 2tr in next st, 2dc in next st, (1hdc, 1sc) in top ch of 2ch.

Fasten off.

STEM

Using A, make a 6in (15cm) long ch, miss 1ch, ss in each remaining ch. Fasten off.

FINISHING Join ends of first and second rows of petals, insert this tube in the tube formed by the sepals and catch together lightly. Attach the stem to the base of the flower.

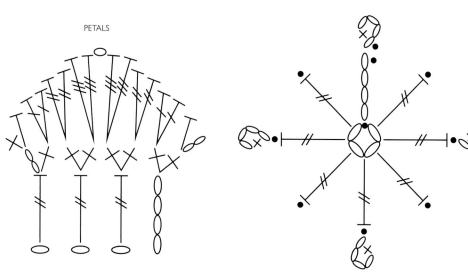

PETALS

SEPALS

54 MARSH MARIGOLD
directory view page 27

Yarn DK cotton in green (A), 2 strands of fine tapestry yarn in yellow (B)

METHOD

STEM
Using A, make 30ch, miss 2ch, ss in back strand of next 28ch. Do not break yarn.

SEPALS
3ch, ss in last of 28ch, 2ch, ss in first ch of 3ch.
Work into these two ch sp from the outside as if they were a ring.

1st round [1sc, 5ch, 1sc] 3 times in 3-ch sp, [1sc, 5ch, 1sc] twice in 2-ch sp. 5 loops. Pull loops forward in order to work behind them.

2nd round [1ch, miss 1sc, 1sc in next sc] 5 times, 1ch, ss in first ch. Fasten off. Turn.

PETALS
Change to B and work around the inside of the ring of sts made in the last round.

3rd round [Ss in next sc, 3ch, 3tr in same sc, 3ch, ss in same sc] 5 times, ss in first sc. 5 petals. Fasten off.

FINISHING Using B, make a small pom-pom to cover the green center of the flower.

55 PRIMULA
directory view page 27

Yarn DK yarn (split into 2 strands) in green (A), yellow (B), and pale yellow (C)

METHOD

FLOWER
Using A and leaving a long end, make 4ch, join with ss into a ring.

1st round 4ch, 4tr in ring, using B ss in top ch of 4ch. 5 sts. This forms a tube with WS of sts to the outside. Now, using B, work around top of tube.

2nd round (RS) 2ch, 2sc in ss, 3sc in each of next 4tr, using C ss in top ch of 2ch. 15 sts. Continue with C.

3rd round * 3ch, 1tr in ss, 1dc in next sc, 1ch, 1tr in next sc, 3ch, ss in same sc as tr, ss in next sc; repeat from * 4 times more, working last ss in ss of 2nd round.

STEM
Insert hook in base of first round, pull through long end of A, make 6ch, miss 1ch, ss in each of next 5ch. Fasten off.

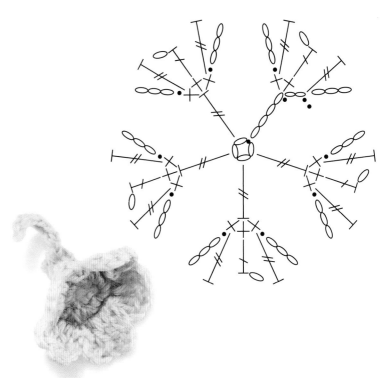

56 OX-EYE DAISY
directory view page 27

Yarn DK yarn in yellow (A), white (B), and green (C)

57 CLOVER LEAF
directory view page 28

Yarn DK yarn in pale green (A) and dark green (B)

METHOD

FLOWER
Using A, make a slip ring (see page 18).
1st round (RS) 1ch, 10sc in ring, pull end to close ring, ss in 1ch. 11 sts. Fasten off.
2nd round Working in front strand only of sc, join B in one sc, * 6ch, miss 2ch, 1hdc in next ch, 1dc in each of next 2ch, 1sc in next ch, ss in front strand of same sc below, ss in front strand of next sc; repeat from *, ending ss in front strand of first sc. 11 petals. Fasten off.

BASE AND STEM
Fasten off ends. Turn flower over and join C in back strand of a sc in ring. Working each st in back strand, 3ch, [dc dec in next 2 sts] 5 times, ss in top ch of 3ch, 1sc in top of a dc on opposite side of group, make 24ch, miss 1ch, ss in each remaining ch. Fasten off.

METHOD

1st round Using A, make 15ch, miss 4ch, 1sc in next ch, [3ch, 1sc in same ch as before] twice, turn.
2nd round (RS) 1ch, (3dc, 1sc) in first ch sp, (1sc, 3dc, 1sc) in each of next 2 ch sp, ss in same ch as 3sc of first round, ss in each of 10ch of stem. Fasten off. Do not turn.
3rd round Using B, join yarn in center of first ch sp, 1ch, * (1sc, 2dc) in first dc, (1dc, 1ch, ss, 1ch, 1dc) in 2nd dc, (2dc, 1sc) in 3rd dc, miss 1sc, insert hook in ch sp below, yrh, pull loop through, insert hook in next ch sp, yrh, pull loop through, yrh, pull yarn through all 3 loops on hook; repeat from * once, (1sc, 2dc) in next dc, (1dc, 1ch, ss, 1ch, 1dc) in next dc, (2dc, 1sc) in last dc, 1sc in 3rd ch sp. Fasten off.

Specific symbols
⌣ work in ch sp
⋀ sc decrease in 2 ch sp

58 OAK LEAF

directory view page 29

Yarn DK yarn in olive (A) and lime (B)

METHOD

Using A, make 23ch.
1st row (RS) Miss 2ch, (1dc, 3tr, 1dc, 1sc)
in next ch, miss 1ch, (1sc, 1dc) in next ch,
3tr in next ch, (1dc, 1sc) in next ch, miss 1ch,
(1dc, 1tr) in next ch, 3dtr in next ch, (1tr, 1dc)
in next ch, miss 1ch, (1sc, 3dc, 1sc) in next ch,
ss in each of next 8ch, 1sc in each of last 2ch.
Fasten off.
2nd row (RS) Rejoin A in single strand of ch
that forms base of last group, 2ch, (3dc, 1sc)
in same ch, miss 1ch, (1dc, 1tr) in next ch,
3dtr in next ch, (1tr, 1dc) in next ch, miss 1ch,
(1sc, 1dc) in next ch, 3tr in next ch, (1dc, 1sc)
in next ch, miss 1ch and base of first group,
ss in next ch. Fasten off.
3rd row (RS) Join B in first ch of 2nd row,
1ch, 2sc in each of 3dc, ss in each of 1sc and
1dc, 1sc in tr, 2sc in each of 3dtr, 1sc in tr, ss in
each of 1dc and 1sc, 1sc in dc, 2sc in each of
3tr, 1sc in dc, ss in sc, miss ss, ss in 23rd ch,
2sc in dc, 2sc in each of 3tr, 2sc in dc, ss in
each of next 2sc, 1sc in dc, 2sc in each of 3tr,
1sc in dc, ss in each of 1sc and 1dc, 1sc in tr,
2sc in each of 3dtr, 1sc in tr, ss in each of 1dc
and 1sc, 2sc in each of 3dc, ss in sc.
Fasten off.

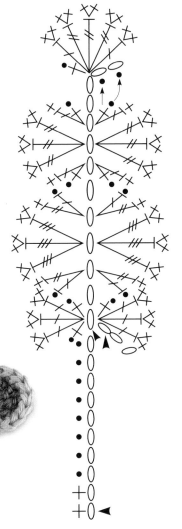

59 NETTLE LEAF

directory view page 29

Yarn DK cotton

METHOD

Make 11ch.
1st row (RS) Miss 1ch, ss in each of next 6ch, miss 3ch,
(6tr, 3dtr, 6tr) in next ch, ss in same ch as last
ss of stem, turn.
2nd row 1ch, miss 1tr, (1sc, 1 picot) in each of next 5tr,
(1dc, 1 picot, 1dc) in first dtr, (1tr, 1 picot, 1tr) in next dtr,
(1dc, 1 picot, 1dc) in next dtr, (1picot, 1sc) in each of next
5tr, ss in last tr. Fasten off.

Specific stitch **picot** 2ch, miss 1ch, ss in next ch

60 STRAWBERRY LEAF
directory view page 37

Yarn DK yarn

METHOD

LEAF (make 3)
Make 8ch.
1st round Miss 1ch, 1sc in next ch, 1hdc in next ch, 1dc in next ch, 2tr in next ch, 1dc in next ch, 1hdc in next ch, 1sc in last ch, 2ch, working into remaining strands of ch: 1sc in next ch, 1hdc in next ch, 1dc in next ch, 2tr in next ch, 1dc in next ch, 1hdc in next ch, 1sc in last ch, join with ss in first sc.
2nd round 1ch, 1sc in each sc, hdc and dc of previous round, 2sc in each tr and 2sc in 2ch sp, ending 1sc in ss at end of 1st round, join with ss in first sc. 23 sc.
3rd round 1ch, * 1sc in next sc, 2ch, miss 1ch, ss in next ch; repeat from * to end, join with ss in first sc. Fasten off.
BRANCHED STALK
Make 18ch. Working in back strand of each ch, miss 1ch, 1sc in each of next 4ch, 7ch, miss 1ch, 1sc in each of next 6ch; 5ch, miss 1ch, 1sc in each of next 4ch, 1sc in each of next 13ch.
FINISHING Stitch one leaf on to each branch of the stalk, overlapping the base of the leaf with about ⅟₁₆in (2mm) of stalk.

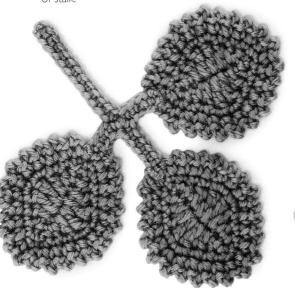

61 STRAWBERRY
directory view page 37

Yarn DK cotton in red (A) and green (B)
Extras Stranded cotton to match strawberry, yellow glass beads, batting

METHOD

Note The strawberry is worked in continuous rounds. Mark the first st of every round (see page 20).

Using A, make 2ch.
1st round Miss 1ch, 6sc in next ch.
2nd round [1sc in next sc, 2sc in next sc] 3 times. 9 sts.
3rd round [1sc in each of next 2sc, 2sc in next sc] 3 times. 12 sts.
4th round 1sc in each sc.
5th round [1sc in each of next 3sc, 2sc in next sc] 3 times. 15 sts.
6th round [1sc in each of next 4sc, 2sc in next sc] 3 times. 18 sts.
7th round 1sc in each sc.
8th round [1sc in each of next 5sc, 2sc in next sc] 3 times. 21 sts.
9th round [1sc in each of next 6sc, 2sc in next sc] 3 times. 24 sts.
10th round 1sc in each sc.
11th round [2-st sc decrease] to end of round. 12 sts.
At this point stitch beads on to the RS of the strawberry using two strands of thread and positioning the beads randomly across the surface. Fasten off the thread securely. Stuff the strawberry firmly and continue.
12th round [2-st sc decrease] to end. 6 sts. Fasten off.
Stitch from side to side of the strawberry to close the opening, tightening each stitch before making the next one.
CALYX
Using B, make 8ch.
1st row (RS) Miss 1ch, 1sc in each ch to end. 7 sc.
2nd row 1ch, * 1sc in next sc, 5ch, miss 1ch, 1sc in each of next 4ch, ss into sc at base of ch; repeat from * to end. Fasten off. With RS to inside, roll calyx and secure with a couple of stitches, stitch to top of strawberry.

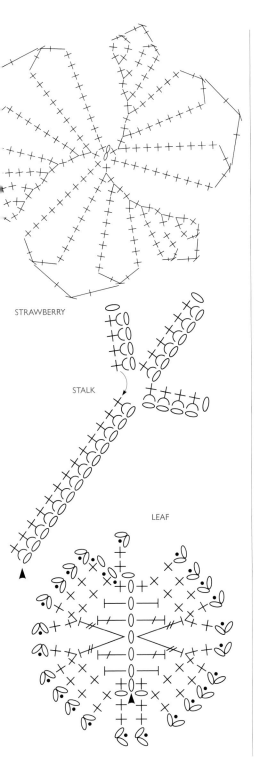

STRAWBERRY

STALK

LEAF

62 LIME AND LEAF
directory view page 36

Yarn DK yarn in lime green (A), dark green (B), and brown (C)
Extra Batting

METHOD

Note The lime is worked in continuous rounds without joining. Use a marker to count rounds (see page 20).

LIME
Using A, make 2ch.
1st round (RS) Miss 1ch, 6sc in next ch. 6 sts.
2nd round 2sc in each sc. 12 sts.
3rd round As 2nd round. 24 sts.
4th and 5th rounds 1sc in each st.
6th round [1sc in next st, 2sc in next st] 12 times. 36 sts.
7th–16th rounds 1sc in each st.
17th round [1sc in next st, sc decrease in next 2 sts] 12 times. 24 sts.
18th and 19th rounds 1sc in each st. At this point, stuff the lime very firmly and then continue.
20th round [2-st sc decrease] to end. 12 sts.
21st round As 20th round. 6 sts.
22nd round 1sc in each st. Fasten off.
LEAF (make 2)
Using B, make 21ch.
1st round (RS) Miss 1ch, working in single strand of each ch, ss in each of next 2ch, 1sc in each of next 2ch, 1hdc in each of next 2ch, 1dc in each of next 8ch, 1hdc in each of next 2ch, 1sc in each of next 2ch, ss in each of last 2ch. 20 sts, excluding 1ch. Working in single strand along opposite side of ch, 1ch, ss in each of next 2ch, 1sc in each of next 2ch, 1hdc in each of next 2ch, 1dc in each of next 8ch, 1hdc in each of next 2ch, 1sc in each of next 2ch, ss in each of last 2ch, join with ss in 1ch. 20 sts, excluding 1ch.
2nd round * Ss in each of first 2 sts, 1sc in each of next 2 sts, 1hdc in each of next 12 sts, 1sc in each of next 2 sts, ss in each

of next 2 sts; repeat from * along opposite side of leaf, join with ss in first ss. Fasten off.
BRANCHING STEM
Using C, make 23ch. Miss 1ch, 1sc in each of next 7ch, 12ch, miss 1ch, 1sc each of next 8ch, 9ch, miss 1ch, 1sc in each of next 8ch, 1sc in each of next 18ch. Fasten off.
FINISHING Stitch the lime on to the first branch worked, overlapping the stem end by about ⅜in (1cm). Stitch one leaf on to each of the remaining two branches.

63 OLIVES
directory view page 36

Yarn DK yarn in dark olive (A) and light gray-green (B)

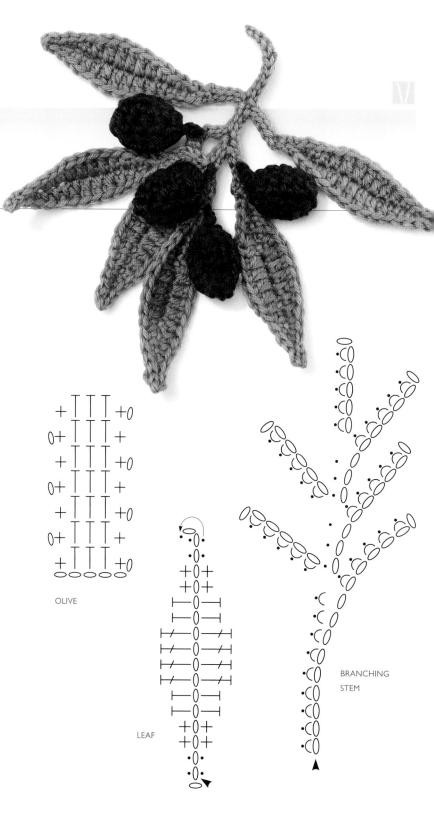

METHOD

Note Either side of olive piece can be used as RS.

OLIVE (make 4)
Using A, make 6ch.
1st row Miss 1ch, 1sc in next ch, 1hdc in each of next 3ch, 1sc in next ch.
2nd row 1ch, 1sc in first sc, 1hdc in each of next 3hdc, 1sc in next sc.
Repeat 2nd row 5 times more. Fasten off.
Fold olive into tube. Join seam, stitch across end, turn to RS. Stuff olive firmly with the same yarn, then close the top, using the yarn end to make 3ch for stalk.

LEAF (make 6)
Using B, make 17ch. Miss 1ch, working in single strand along edge of ch, ss in each of next 2ch, 1sc in each of next 2ch, 1hdc in each of next 2ch, 1dc in each of next 4ch, 1hdc in each of next 2ch, 1sc in each of next 2ch, ss in each of last 2ch. 16 sts. 1ch, working in single edge strand again, ss in each of next 2ch, 1sc in each of next 2ch, 1hdc in each of next 2ch, 1dc in each of next 4ch, 1hdc in each of next 2ch, 1sc in each of next 2ch, ss in each of last 2ch. 16 sts. Join with ss in first ss. Fasten off.

BRANCHING STEM Using B, make 15ch. Miss 1ch, working in back strand of each ch, ss in each of next 5ch, 9ch, miss 1ch, ss in each of next 5ch, 9ch, miss 1ch, ss in each of next 5ch, 6ch, miss 1ch, ss in each of next 5ch, ss in each of next 3ch, 6ch, miss 1ch, ss in each of next 5ch, ss in each of next 3ch, 6ch, miss 1ch, ss in each of next 5ch, ss in next 9ch. Fasten off.

FINISHING Stitch one leaf on to each branch of the stem. Stitch the olives randomly on to the stems.

Specific symbol
⌒ Ss in back strand of ch

OLIVE

LEAF

BRANCHING
STEM

64 RED BELL PEPPER

directory view page 38

Yarn DK yarn in red (A) and green (B)
Extra Batting

METHOD

SEGMENT (make 3)
Using A, make 26ch.
1st row (RS) Miss 1ch, 1sc in each of next 25ch. 25 sts.
2nd row 1ch, ss in first sc, 1sc in each of next 4sc, 1hdc in each of next 4sc, 1dc in each of next 13sc, 1hdc in next sc, 1sc in next sc, ss in last sc.
3rd row 1ch, ss in ss, 1sc in next sc, 1hdc in next hdc, 1dc in each of next 13dc, 1hdc in each of next 4hdc, 1sc in each of next 4sc, ss in ss.
4th row 1ch, 1sc in each st. 25 sc.
5th row 1ch, ss in first sc, 1sc in next sc, 1hdc in next sc, 1dc in each of next 13sc, 1hdc in each of next 4sc, 1sc in each of next 4sc, ss in next sc.
6th row 1ch, ss in ss, 1sc in each of next 4sc, 1hdc in each of next 4hdc, 1dc in each of next 13dc, 1hdc in next hdc, 1sc in next sc, ss in ss.
7th row As 4th row.
8th–12th rows As 2nd–6th rows.
13th row 1ch, 1sc in each st. 25 sc. Fasten off.
FINISHING Right sides together, pin long edges of segments to make a tube. Backstitch them, taking stitches through both strands of adjoining stitches. Aligning seams, fold each narrow end of segments and oversew edges together.
Turn to RS and stuff.

STALK
With RS facing, join B to edge of opening at top of bell pepper, 1ch, making first sc in same st as 1ch, work 4sc in each segment and a 2-st sc decrease over sts at either side of seams, then ss in first sc. 15sc.
1st and 2nd rounds 1ch, 1sc in each sc, ss in first sc.
3rd round 1ch, 1sc, [2-st sc decrease] 7 times, ss in 1sc. 8dc. Omitting 1ch, work in continuous rounds until narrow part of stalk measures ¾in (2cm). Break yarn and stitch across top of stalk to close.

65 CORN
directory view page 39

Yarn DK yarn in soft yellow (A), bright green (B), and mid green (C), tapestry wool in pale yellow
Extra Batting

METHOD

Note **3-st bobble** make 1dc, omitting last wrap (see page 13) to leave 2 loops on hook. Work 2 more incomplete dc into the same st (4 loops on the hook), then pull yarn through all loops to complete bobble. On the next row, work 1sc in the top of the bobble. **2-st bobble** is similar, but work only 2 incomplete dc (3 loops on the hook) before pulling yarn through to complete bobble.

CORN
Using A, make 22ch.
Set-up row Miss 1ch, 1sc in each of 21ch. 21sc.
1st row (WS) 1ch, 1sc in first st, [3-st bobble in next st, 1sc in next st] 10 times.
2nd row 1ch, 1sc in each st.
Repeat 1st and 2nd rows 8 times more.
19th, 21st, and 23rd rows 1ch, 1sc in first st, [2-st bobble in next st, 1sc in next st] 10 times.
20th and 22nd rows 1ch, 1sc in each st.
24th row Ss in first 2sc, 1ch, 1sc in st below, 1sc in each st, omitting last st. 19sc.
25th row 1ch, 1sc in first st, [2-st bobble in next st, 1sc in next st] to end.
26th and 27th rows As 24th and 25th rows. 17sc.
28th and 29th rows As 24th and 25th rows. 15sc.
30th and 31st rows As 24th and 25th rows. 13sc.
32nd row 1ch, miss first st, [2-st sc decrease] to end. 6 sts. Fasten off.
WS facing, fold corn in half lengthwise.
Stitch across top and down seam.
Turn corn to RS and stuff firmly.

STALK
Join B to base of corn at seam, 1ch, work 21sc evenly around base, join with ss in first sc.
2nd and 3rd rounds 1ch, 1sc in each dc, ss in first sc.
4th round 3ch, 2-st dc decrease, [3-st dc decrease] to end of round, join with a ss in top ch of 3ch. Gather edge of last round tightly to close gap at center.
LEAVES (make 1 with B, 2 with C)
Make 10ch.
1st row Miss 1ch, working into strand that lies behind each ch, work 1sc in each of 9ch. 9sc.
2nd row 1ch, 1sc in each sc.
3rd row (RS) 3ch (counts as 1dc), 1dc in st below, [1dc in next st, 2dc in next st] 4 times. 14dc.
4th row 1ch, 1sc in each dc. 14sc.
5th row 3ch, miss 1sc, 1dc in each sc.
6th row 1ch, 1sc in each dc. Repeat 5th and 6th rows 10 times more.

27th row 3ch, 2-st dc decrease, 1dc in each sc to last 3 sts, 2-st dc decrease, 1dc in last st.
28th row 1ch, 1sc in each dc. Repeat 27th and 28th rows 3 times. 6 sts.
35th row 3ch, [2-st dc decrease] twice, 1dc in last sc. 4 sts.
36th row 1ch, [2-st sc decrease] twice. Fasten off.

SILK
Cut fourteen 8in (20cm) lengths of tapestry wool. Thread each length in a yarn needle and insert randomly around top of corn, aligning ends, and securing in place with an overhand knot. When all the lengths have been attached, trim to required length, and fray out the ends of each.

66 CHILI
directory view page 36

Yarn 4-ply yarn in red (A) and green (B))

METHOD

Using A, make a slip ring (see page 18).
1st round (RS) 3ch, 3dc in ring, pull end to close ring, ss in top ch of 3ch. 4 sts.
2nd round 3ch, 2dc in next dc, 1dc in next dc, 2dc in next dc, ss in top ch of 3ch. 6 sts.
3rd round 3ch, 2dc in next dc, [1dc in next dc, 2dc in next dc] twice, ss in top ch of 3ch. 9 sts.
4th round 3ch, 1dc in next dc, 2dc in next dc, [1dc in each of next 2 dc, 2dc in next dc] twice, ss in top of 3ch. 12 sts.
5th, 6th, 7th, and 8th rounds 3ch, 1dc in each of next 11dc, ss in top ch of 3ch.
9th round 1ch, sc decrease in next 2dc, [1sc in next dc, sc decrease in next 2dc] 3 times, with B, ss in 1ch. 8 sts. Continue with B.
10th round 1ch, ss in each of next 7 sts, ss in 1ch. Without breaking yarn, insert spare yarn A as filling.
11th round 1ch, working in back strand of each st, sc decrease in next 2 sts, 1sc in next st, [sc decrease in next 2 sts] twice, ss in 1ch. 5 sts. Do not break yarn.
STEM
9ch, miss 2ch, 1sc in next ch, ss in each of next 6ch. Fasten off and use end to secure base of stem.

FINISHING Center B leaf over seam on corn, aligning straight end of leaf with base of stalk and placing WS of leaf to RS of corn. Leaving chain edge at base of leaf free, stitch in place through base of each sc on 1st row. Repeat with other two leaves, overlapping first leaf by about ⅝in (1.5cm). Arrange leaves, pin in place, then secure leaf edges at back of corn with rows of stitches worked in matching yarn, making sure the stitches go through both leaf and corn.

67 YELLOW SQUASH

directory view page 38

Yarn DK yarn in soft yellow (A) and light brown (B)
Extra Batting

METHOD

Note On body, stitches are worked through both loops, single back loops, or single front loops on different rows.

BODY

Using A, make 25ch.

Set-up row (RS) Miss 1ch, 1sc in each of next 5ch, 1hdc in next ch, 1dc in each of next 12ch, 1hdc in next ch, 1sc in each of next 5ch. 24 sts, excluding 1ch.

1st row 1ch, working into back loops only of previous row, 1sc in each of next 5sc, 1hdc in hdc, 1dc in each of next 12dc, 1hdc in hdc, 1sc in each of next 5 sts.

2nd row 1ch, working into both loops of previous row, 1sc in each of next 5sc, 1hdc in hdc, 1dc in each of next 12dc, 1hdc in hdc, 1sc in each of next 5 sts.

3rd row 1ch, working into front loops only of previous row, 1sc in each of next 5sc, 1hdc in hdc, 1dc in each of next 12dc, 1hdc in hdc, 1sc in each of next 5sc.

4th row As 2nd row.

Repeat 1st–4th rows 8 times, then repeat 1st–3rd rows once more.

WS facing, fold body to form a tube, aligning edge of last row with starting chain.

Ss through both layers and turn tube to RS.

STALK

With RS facing, join B to one end of tube, 1ch, work round of sc (1sc for every 2 row ends), join with ss in first sc. 20sc.

Next round 1ch, 1sc in each sc, ss in first sc.

Next round 1ch, [2-st sc decrease] to end, ss in first 2-st sc decrease. 10 sts.

Begin working sc continuously (do not join rounds). When stalk measures ⅝in (1.5cm),

work a round of 2-st sc decrease, fasten off, and stitch across top of stalk to close.

Cut ten 10in (25cm) lengths of A. Secure one end of each length on WS of squash below stalk where grooves form between 1st and 4th rows (note that first groove is formed between 1st row and set-up row). Bring each length through to RS, work row of running stitches along groove, pull yarn end gently to tighten up running stitches and accentuate groove, then finish off each end securely.

Stuff squash body lightly, forming it first into a doughnut shape, then stuffing center of doughnut.

BASE

Using B, make 4ch and join with ss into a ring.

1st round 1ch, 10sc in ring, ss in first sc.

2nd round 1ch, [1sc in next sc, 2sc in next sc] to end, ss in first sc. 15 sc.

3rd round 1ch, [1sc in each of next 2sc, 2sc in next sc] to end, ss in first sc. 20sc. Continue with A.

4th round 3ch, 1 dc in st below, 2dc in each sc, ss in top ch of 3ch. 40 sts.

5th round 1ch, 1sc in each dc, ss in first sc. Fasten off.

Lay base over gap at bottom of squash. Leaving front loop of each sc free, sew in place.

68 STRIPED SQUASH
directory view page 39

Yarn DK yarn in pale green (A), mid green (B), and light brown (C)
Extra Batting

METHOD

Note Do not break off yarn at each color change, but carry yarn not in use up side of work. Change color by working last wrap (see page 13) of last st of row in new color before turning to work next row.

BODY

Using A, make 25ch.
Set-up row (RS) Miss 1ch, 1sc in each of next 4ch, 1hdc in each of next 2ch, 1dc in each of next 12ch, 1hdc in each of next 2ch, 1sc in each of next 4ch.
1st row Using A, 1ch, 1sc in each of next 4sc, 1hdc in each of next 2hdc, 1dc in each of next 12dc, 1hdc in each of next 2hdc, 1sc in each of next 4sc. Change to B.
2nd row Using B, 1ch, 1sc in each of next 4sc, 1hdc in each of next 2hdc, 1dc in each of next 12dc, 1hdc in each of next 2hdc, 1sc in each of next 4sc.
3rd row Using B, 1ch, 1sc in each st of previous row. 24sc. Change to A.
4th row Using A, 1ch, 1sc in each of next 4sc, 1hdc in each of next 2sc, 1dc in each of next 12sc, 1hdc in each of next 2sc, 1sc in each of next 4sc.
Repeat 1st–4th rows 8 times, then repeat 1st–3rd rows once more.
WS facing, fold body to form a tube, aligning edge of last row with starting chain. Ss through both layers. Fasten off. With A, work running stitches around the end of the tube where you changed yarns, draw up the stitches to close the tube, and fasten off securely. Turn body to RS. Stuff squash body fairly firmly so that it will stand upright on the gathered base.

STALK

With RS facing and using A, work sc around top of squash, starting at seam and working 1sc into top of each stripe, join with ss in first sc. 20 sc.
1st round 1ch, 1sc in each sc, ss in first sc. Repeat first round once.
Change to C and repeat first round twice.
Next round 1ch, [2-st sc decrease] to end of round, join with ss in first 2-st sc decrease. Adding more stuffing as required, work sc continuously (do not join rounds). When stalk measures ⅝in (1.5cm), work a round of 2-st sc decrease. Fasten off yarn, leaving top of stalk open.

69 APPLE
directory view page 37

Yarn DK yarn in white (A), apple green (B), and dark green (C), 4-ply yarn in brown (D)
Hooks Two crochet hooks, one a size smaller than the other
Extras Heavy nonwoven interfacing, stranded embroidery cotton to match B, batting

METHOD

FRONT
Using larger hook and A, make 8ch.
1st round Miss 1ch, working in a single strand of each ch, 1sc in next ch, 1hdc in next ch, 1dc in next ch, 2tr in next ch, 1dc in next ch, 1hdc in next ch, 1sc and 1ss in last ch. Working in single strands along opposite side, 1sc in first ch, 1hdc in next ch, 1dc in next ch, 2tr in next ch, 1dc in next ch, 1hdc in next ch, 1sc in last ch, ss in first sc. 17 sts.
2nd round 1ch, 1sc in st below, 1sc in each st of previous round, working 2sc in each tr and 2sc into ss at center, ss in first sc. 22 sts.
3rd round 1ch, 1sc in st below, 1dc in next st, 3tr in next st, 2tr in next st, 3tr in next st, 1dc in next st, 2hdc in each of next 3 sts, 1hdc in next st, (1sc, 1ss) in next st, (1ss, 1sc) in next st, 1hdc in next st, 2hdc in each of next 3 sts, 1dc in next st, 3tr in next st, 2tr in next st, 3tr in next st, 1dc in next st, 1sc in next st, ss in first sc. 40 sts.
4th round (1sc, 1hdc) in next st, 2dc in next st, 3dc in each of next 2 sts, 2dc in each of next 3 sts, 1hdc in each of next 3 sts, 1sc in each of next 8 sts, ss in each of next 2 sts, 1sc in each of next 8 sts, 1hdc in each of next 3 sts, 2dc in each of next 3 sts, 3dc in each of next 2 sts, 2dc in next st, (1hdc, 1sc) in next st, ss in last st, ss in ss at end of last row. Fasten off.
5th round Join B in any sc along side edge of piece, 1ch, 1sc in same st, 1sc in each st of previous round, working (miss one st, ss in each of next 2 sts, miss next st) in 4 sts at center of top of apple and (ss in next st, miss one st, ss in next st) at center of base of apple, join with ss in first sc. Fasten off.
BACK
Using larger hook and B, join yarn at top, make 3ch.
1st row (RS) Miss 1ch, 2sc in each of next 2ch. 4sc.
2nd row 1ch, 2sc in first sc, 1sc in each of next 2sc, 2sc in next sc. 6sc.
3rd row 1ch, 2sc in each of first 2sc, 1sc in each of next 2sc, 2sc in each of next 2sc. 10sc.

4th row 1ch, 2sc in each of first 2sc, 1sc in each of next 6sc, 2sc in each of next 2sc. 14sc.
5th row 1ch, 1sc in each sc.
6th row 1ch, 2sc in first sc, 1sc in each of next 12sc, 2sc in next sc. 16sc.
7th row As 5th row.
8th row 1ch, 1sc in each of first 3sc, 2sc in next sc, 1sc in each of next 3sc, 2sc in each of next 2sc, 1sc in each of next 3sc, 2sc in next sc, 1sc in each of next 3sc. 20sc.
9th row 1ch, 1sc in each of first 4sc, 2sc in next sc, 1sc into each of next 4sc, 2 sc in each of next 2sc, 1sc in each of next 4sc, 2sc in next sc, 1sc in each of next 4sc. 24sc.
10th–15th rows As 5th row.
16th row 1ch, 1sc in first sc, 2-st sc decrease, 1sc in each sc to last 3 sts, 2-st sc decrease, 1sc in next sc. 22 sts.
17th row As 16th row. 20 sts.

18th row 1ch, 1sc in each of first 3sc, 2-st sc decrease, 1sc in each of next 3sc, [2-st sc decrease] twice, 1sc in each of next 3sc, 2-st sc decrease, 1sc in each of next 3sc. 16 sts.

19th row As 16th row. 14sts.

20th row As 5th row.

21st–24th rows As 16th row. 6 sts.

25th row 1ch, 1sc in first sc, [2-st sc decrease] twice, 1sc in next sc. 4 sts. Fasten off.

STALK

Using larger hook and C, make 9ch. Miss 1ch, 1sc in each of next 4ch, ss in each of next 4ch. Fasten off.

PIPS (make 2)

Using smaller hook and D, make 2ch. Miss 1ch, without completing last wrap (see page 13) make 3dc in next ch, yrh, pull yarn through all 4 loops on hook. Fasten off. Tighten each yarn end to form a tiny bobble.

FINISHING Press front to shape. Place front WS down on interfacing and baste to secure. Using 4 strands of embroidery thread, back stitch around the front, following the base of stitches worked in B. Work a row of back stitches down the center, then work the same stitch in an oval shape between the stitches of 2nd and 3rd rounds. Carefully trim away the interfacing close to the edge. Using yarn ends, sew pips in place either side of the central stitched line, then sew the base of the stalk to the top of the front. Beginning at the top near the stalk, WS together, oversew front to back aligning edges and taking each stitch through edge of back and behind outer round of sc on front. Leave a small opening on the second side, insert batting, then continue stitching up to the top.

70 SNAIL
directory view page 31

Yarn Space dyed 4-ply wool in beige and browns (A) and 3-ply wool in brown (B)
Hooks Two crochet hooks, one a size smaller than the other
Extras Batting, fine wire, 2 small black beads

METHOD

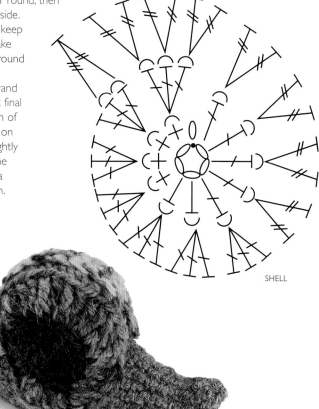

SHELL (first side)
Using larger hook and A, make 5ch, join with ss into a ring.
1st round (RS) 1ch, 4sc, 2hdc, 5dc in ring. ** Now work in continuous rounds without joining and working into the back strand of each st, 3dc in each of next 7 sts, 2tr in each of next 7 sts, without working the last wrap of each st (see page 13), 1tr in next st, 1dtr in next st, yrh and pull yarn through all 4 loops on hook. Fasten off.
SHELL (second side)
As first side, but working all sts from ** in the front strand of each st and noting that the back of the work will be the RS.
BODY
Using smaller hook and B, make a slip ring (see page 18).
1st round (WS) 2ch, 5sc in ring, pull end to close ring, ss in top ch of 2ch. 6 sts. Marking the beginning of each round (see page 20), work in continuous rounds of sc without joining, and working in the back strand of each st. Work 3 rounds straight.
5th round [1sc in each of next 2 sts, 2sc in next st] twice. 8 sts.
6th round [1sc in next st, 2sc in next st] 4 times. 12 sts.
7th round [1sc in next st] 12 times.
8th round [1sc in each of next 2 sts, 2sc in next st] 4 times. 16 sts.
Turn work inside out (RS is now outside), continue working with WS facing, working into back strand of each st.
9th round [1sc in next st, 2sc in next st] 8 times. 24 sts.
10th round [1sc in next st] 24 times.
11th round [1sc in each of next 3 sts, 2sc in next st] 6 times. 30 sts.

Work 6 rounds straight. Fill the body with batting and continue to fill as you crochet.
Decrease round [1sc in next st, sc decrease in next 2 sts] 10 times. 20 sts.
Work 4 rounds straight.
FIRST HORN
Make 10ch, miss 2ch, ss in each of next 8ch. 1sc in each of next 3sc, make second horn to match, then complete the round. Ensuring horns protrude on RS, work 1 round, then a part round, ending at underside. Shaping the body carefully to keep underside flat, finish stuffing, take yarn end through top of last round of sts and draw up.
FINISHING Leaving outer strand of each st free, and starting at final st of each piece, join top seam of shell for 15 sts, catch it down on either side of the body and lightly stuff with spare yarn. Insert fine wire into the horns and sew a bead on the end of each horn.

Specific symbol
⌒ work into back strand of st on first side of shell, but work into front strand of st on second side

SHELL

71 BEETLE
directory view page 30

Yarn Metallic yarn (used double)
Extras 2 beads, strong sewing thread in a darker color

METHOD

BODY (Worked in one round, RS facing)
Using yarn double, make 9ch, miss 2ch, 3sc in next ch, dc decrease in next 2ch, decrease in next 2ch, dc decrease in next 2ch, 2ch, ss in last ch worked into, 2ch, working in remaining strands of original ch, dc decrease in next 2ch, tr decrease in next 2ch, dc decrease in next 2ch, ss in top ch of 9ch. Fasten off.

UNDERSIDE
Using yarn double, make a slip ring (see page 18). 3ch, 7dc in ring, pull end to tighten ring, ss in top ch of 3ch. Fasten off.

FINISHING Concave side to the inside, stitch the underside to the body, filling with a little spare yarn if necessary. Using sewing thread double, back stitch along the center back line of chain and around the cluster forming the head. Sew on 2 beads for eyes.

72 LADYBUG
directory view page 31

Yarn 4-ply yarn in black (A), red (B), and white (C)

METHOD

BODY
Using A, make 3ch.
1st row (RS) Miss 2ch, making the last wrap (see page 13) of the sc with B, (2dc, 1sc) in next ch. 4 sts.
Continue with B.
2nd row 2ch, (1dc, 1tr) in first dc, (1tr, 1dc) in 2nd dc, 1sc in top ch of 3ch. 6 sts.
3rd row 3ch, 1dc in dc, [2tr in tr] twice, 1dc in dc, 1sc in top ch of 2ch. 8 sts. Fasten off.

UNDERSIDE
Using A, make 2ch.
1st row Miss 1ch, 2sc in next ch. 3 sts.
2nd row 2ch, 1sc in st below, 1sc in next sc, 2sc in top ch of 2ch. 5 sts.
3rd row 2ch, 1sc in each of next 3sc, 1sc in top ch of 2ch.
4th row 2ch, miss 1sc, 1sc in next sc, miss 1sc, 1sc in top ch of 2ch. 3 sts.
5th row 2ch, miss 1sc, 1sc in top ch of 2ch. 2 sts. Fasten off.

FINISHING Using split yarn for embroidery, stitch 3 spots on either side of body with B. Use C to embroider 3 spots on head. RS facing and using A for head, B for body, use running stitch to join body and underside, stuffing with ends and spare yarn B before closing.

BODY

UNDERSIDE

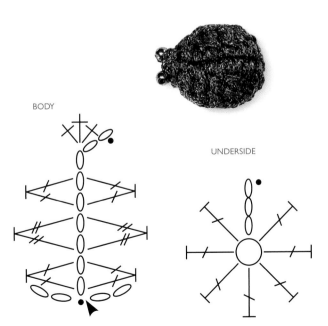

BODY

UNDERSIDE

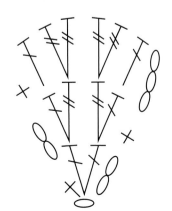

73 FURRY CATERPILLAR
directory view page 31

Yarn Fine mohair
Extras 2 sequins, sewing thread, 16 faceted beads, 14 round beads

METHOD

Make a slip ring (see page 18).
1st round (RS) 3ch, 5dc in ring, pull end to close ring, ss in top ch of 3ch. 6 sts.
2nd round 3ch, working into back loop of st each time, 2dc in next dc, [1dc in next dc, 2dc in next dc] twice, ss in top ch of 3ch. 9 sts.
3rd round 3ch, working into back loop of st each time, 1dc in each of 8dc, ss in top ch of 3ch.
Repeat 3rd round 5 times more, then fill with spare yarn.
9th round 3ch, working into back loop of st each time, [dc decrease in next 2dc] 4 times.
Insert some more filling, then ss in top ch of 3ch.
Fasten off.
FINISHING Close last end and sew on 2 sequins for eyes. For legs, sew pairs of faceted beads either side of ch joins of rounds, using top strand of dc as markers for spacing. With mohair overcast these strands and gather slightly to form the segments of the body. Stitch loops along the back, anchoring each loop with a back st. Sew round beads along each side, one bead to each segment.

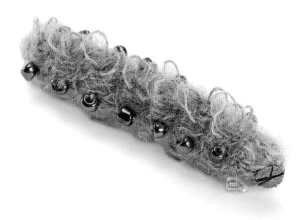

74 SPIDER
directory view page 30

Yarn DK wool
Extras Pipe cleaners, sewing needle, nail varnish or glue

METHOD

HEAD
Make 4ch, miss 3ch, 4dc in next ch, remove hook leaving loop, insert hook in top ch of 4ch then in loop, yrh, pull yarn through firmly. Fasten off and darn in end inside cavity.
BODY
5ch, miss 4ch, 7tr in next ch, turn and ss in top ch of 5ch. Fasten off, leaving an extra long end. Fill cavity with spare yarn then use long end to gather top of sts.
FINISHING Join head to body. Cut the pipe cleaners into four 2⅜in (6cm) lengths. Bind each length with yarn: starting near one end, bind to that end then work back over this to secure the yarn end; bind to the opposite end then thread yarn on to a sewing needle and take it back under the last wraps firmly. Trim ends of yarn and ends of pipe cleaner. Secure ends with nail varnish or glue. Form a shallow X with 2 pipe cleaners, secure it then stitch underneath the body of the spider. Bend the remaining 2 pipe cleaners into U shapes and stitch these, one above and one below the X.

HEAD

BODY

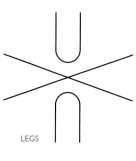

LEGS

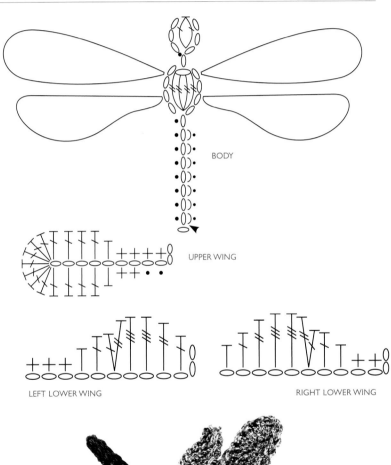

75 DRAGONFLY

directory view page 27

Yarn 4-ply cotton (A) and 4-ply-weight metallic yarn (B)
Extra 2 beads

METHOD

BODY (worked in a single round, RS facing)
Using A, make 12ch. Miss 4ch, 4tr in next ch, remove
hook leaving loop, insert hook in top ch of 4ch then in loop,
yrh, pull yarn through (popcorn made), 4ch, miss 2ch,
2-st dc cluster in next ch, 3ch, ss in first of 4ch, 4ch, ss in
same ch as base of popcorn, ss in each of remaining 7ch,
1ch, working in single remaining strand each time,
ss in each of 7ch. Fasten off.

UPPER WINGS (make 2)
Using B, make 11ch. Miss 2ch, 1sc in each of next 4ch, 1hdc
in next ch, 1dc in each of next 3ch, 9dc in next ch; working
in remaining strand of each ch and enclosing yarn end,
1dc in each of next 3ch, 1hdc in next ch, 1sc in each of
next 2ch, ss in each of next 2ch. Fasten off.

RIGHT LOWER WING (worked in a single row, RS facing)
Using B, make 12ch. Miss 2ch, 1sc in each of next 2ch, 1hdc
in next ch, 1dc in next ch, (1dc, 1tr) in next ch, 1dtr in each
of next 2ch, 1tr in next ch, 1dc in next ch, 1hdc in next ch.
Fasten off.

LEFT LOWER WING (worked in a single row, RS facing)
Using B, make 12ch. Miss 2ch, 1dc in next ch, 1tr in next ch,
1dtr in each of next 2ch, (1tr, 1dc) in next ch, 1dc in next
ch, 1hdc in next ch, 1sc in each of next 3ch. Fasten off.

FINISHING Carefully fasten off ends of right lower wing,
running them back along the set-up chain. Pair upper wings
and join. Do the same with lower wings, noting that the
foundation chain runs along the top edge of the lower
wings. Position them underneath the body and stitch. Join
upper and lower wings with a single invisible st halfway
along. Sew on 2 beads for eyes.

BODY

UPPER WING

LEFT LOWER WING

RIGHT LOWER WING

76 CEP MUSHROOM
directory view page 40

Yarn Single strands of tapestry yarn in beige (A) and yellow ochre or orange (B)
Extra Batting

METHOD

Note If you wish to avoid a ss join between rounds, work continuously, substituting 1sc for 1ch at the beginning and omitting the ss at the end of each round, but mark the rounds with contrast yarn (see page 20).

LARGE MUSHROOM
STALK
Using A, make a slip ring (see page 18).
1st round (RS) 1ch, 7sc in ring, pull end to close ring, ss in 1ch. 8 sts.
2nd round 1ch, 2sc in next sc, [1sc in next sc, 2sc in next sc] 3 times, ss in 1ch. 12 sts.
3rd round 1ch, 2sc in next sc, [1sc in next sc, 2sc in next sc] 5 times, ss in 1ch. 18 sts. **
4th round 1ch, 2sc in next sc, [1sc in next sc, 2sc in next sc] 8 times, ss in 1ch. 27 sts.
5th round 1ch, 1sc in next sc, 2sc in next sc, [1sc in each of next 2sc, 2sc in next sc] 8 times, ss in 1ch. 36 sts.
6th, 7th, and 8th rounds 1ch, 1sc in each sc, ss in 1ch.
9th round 1ch, 1sc in each of next 3sc, sc decrease in next 2sc, [1sc in each of next 4sc, sc decrease in next 2sc] 5 times. 30 sts.
10th and 11th rounds As 6th round.
12th round 1ch, 1sc in each of next 2sc, sc decrease in next 2sc, [1sc in each of next 3sc, sc decrease in next 2sc] 5 times, ss in 1ch. 24 sts.
13th and 14th rounds As 6th round.
15th round 1ch, 1sc in next sc, sc decrease in next 2sc, [1sc in each of next 2sc, sc decrease in next 2sc] 5 times, ss in 1ch. 18 sts.
16th, 17th, 18th, and 19th rounds As 6th round.
20th round 3ch, 1dc in st below, [2dc in next sc] 17 times, ss in top ch of 3ch. 36 sts. Fasten off.
CAP
Using B, make a slip ring.
1st round (RS) 1ch, 5sc in ring, pull end to close ring, ss in 1ch. 6 sts.

2nd round 1ch, 1sc in st below, 2sc in each of next 5sc, ss in 1ch. 12 sts.
3rd round 1ch, 2sc in next sc, [1sc in next sc, 2sc in next sc] 5 times, ss in 1ch. 18 sts.
4th round 1ch, 1sc in next sc, 2sc in next sc, [1sc in each of next 2sc, 2sc in next sc] 5 times, ss in 1ch. 24 sts.
5th round 1ch, 1sc in each of next 2sc, 2sc in next sc, [1sc in each of next 3sc, 2sc in next sc] 5 times, ss in 1ch. 30 sts.
6th round 1ch, 1sc in each of next 3sc, 2sc in next sc, [1sc in each of next 4sc, 2sc in next sc] 5 times, ss in 1ch. 36 sts. ***
7th round 1ch, 1sc in each sc, ss in 1ch.
8th round 1ch, 1sc in each of next 4sc, 2sc in next sc, [1sc in each of next 5sc, 2sc in next sc] 5 times, ss in 1ch. 42 sts.
9th, 10th, and 11th rounds As 7th round.
Turn to work last round on WS.
12th round 1ch, 1sc in each of next 4sc, sc decrease in next 2sc, [1sc in each of next 6sc, sc decrease in next 2sc] 5 times, ss in 1ch. 36 sts. Fasten off.
FINISHING Stuff the stalk. Using B and matching stitch for stitch, take the yarn under the chain edge of the last round of the cap and around the treble stitches of the last round of the stalk. Backstitch the cap to the stalk, stuffing before completing.

SMALL MUSHROOM

STALK Work as larger mushroom stem to **.

4th and 5th rounds 1ch, 1sc in each sc, ss in 1ch.

6th round 1ch, 1sc in each of next 3sc, sc decrease in next 2sc, [1sc in each of next 4sc, sc decrease in next 2sc] twice, ss in 1ch. 15 sts.

7th round As 4th round.

8th round 1ch, 1sc in each of next 2sc, sc decrease in next 2sc, [1sc in each of next 3sc, sc decrease in next 2sc] twice, ss in 1ch. 12 sts.

9th, 10th, and 11th rounds As 4th round.

12th round 3ch, 1dc in st below, [2dc in next sc] 11 times, ss in top ch of 3ch. 24 sts. Fasten off.

CAP Work as larger mushroom cap to ***.

7th and 8th rounds 1ch, 1sc in each sc, ss in 1ch. Turn to work last round on WS.

9th round 1ch, sc decrease in next 2sc, [1sc in next sc, sc decrease in next 2sc] 11 times, ss in 1ch. 24 sts. Fasten off.

FINISHING As for larger mushroom.

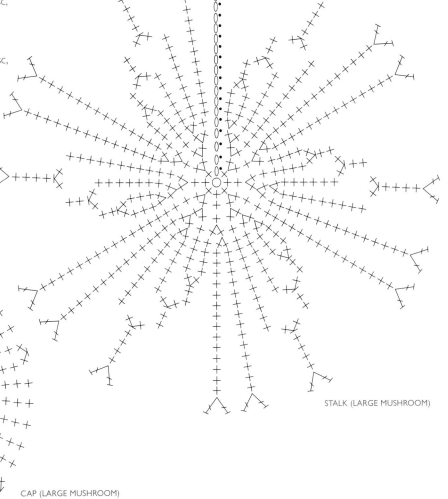

STALK (LARGE MUSHROOM)

CAP (LARGE MUSHROOM)

77 WAXCAP

directory view page 41

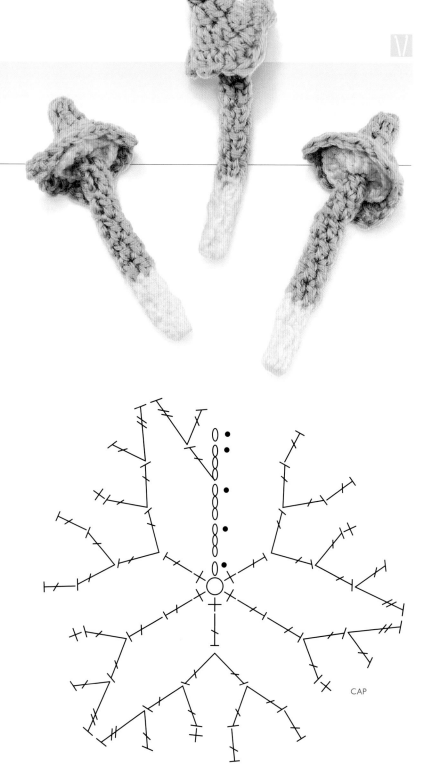

Yarn DK yarn in yellow ocher (A) and white (B)

METHOD

CAP Using A, make a slip ring (see page 18).

1st round (RS) 1ch, 5sc in ring, pull end to close ring, ss in 1ch. 6 sts.

2nd round 3ch, 1dc in each of 5sc, ss in top ch of 3ch.

3rd round 3ch, 2dc in next dc, [1dc in next dc, 2dc in next dc] twice, ss in top ch of 3ch. 9 sts.

4th round 3ch, 1dc in st below, 2dc in each of next 8dc, ss in top ch of 3ch. 18 sts.

5th round 1ch, * (1dc, 1tr) in next dc, (1tr, 1dc) in next dc, 1sc in next dc, 1dc in each of next 2dc, 1sc in next sc; repeat from *, ending 1dc in each of next 2dc, ss in 1ch. Fasten off.

STALK Using B, make 4ch, join with ss into a ring.

1st round (RS) 3ch, enclosing yarn end work 5dc in ring, ss in top ch of 3ch. 6 sts.

2nd round 3ch, 1dc in each of 5dc, ss in top ch of 3ch. Repeat 2nd round once more, making ss with A. Continue with A.

Repeat 2nd round 6 times more, making last ss with B. Continue with B.

10th round 3ch, 2dc in st below, 3dc in each of next 5dc, ss in top ch of 3ch. 18 sts. Fasten off.

FINISHING Press scalloped edge of cap. Use ends as light stuffing for cap, then attach top of stem (gills) by backstitching with B along the inside of the chain edge and catching only half a strand of yarn on the inside of the cap.

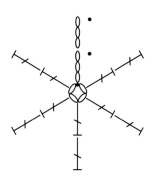

STALK
The chart shows the first two rounds; repeat 2nd round.

CAP

78 CHRISTMAS STAR

directory view page 43

Yarn 4-ply-weight metallic yarn

METHOD

Make a slip ring (see page 18).
1st round (RS) 3ch, 11dc in ring, pull end to close ring, ss in top ch of 3ch. 12 sts.
2nd round 3ch, 1dc in st below, 1trf in next st, [2dc in next st, 1trf in next st] 5 times, ss in top ch of 3ch. 18 sts.
3rd round 5ch, ss in st below, ss in next st, 2ch, 1dc in same st as ss below, 1trf in next st, [1dc in next st, 2ch, ss in same st as dc, ss in next st, 2ch, 1dc in same st as ss below, 1trf in next st] 5 times, ss in 3rd ch of 5ch. Turn.

FIRST POINT
1st row (WS) 3ch, 1trb in next trf, 1dc in dc, turn.
2nd row Miss tr, ss in top ch of 3ch. Fasten off.

SECOND POINT
1st row WS facing, rejoin yarn in first dc of next group of sts, 3ch, 1trb in next trf, 1dc in dc, turn.
2nd row Miss tr, ss in top ch of 3ch. Fasten off.
Repeat second point 4 times.

Specific abbreviations trb tr made from the back around the stem of the st; **trf** tr made from the front around the stem of the st.

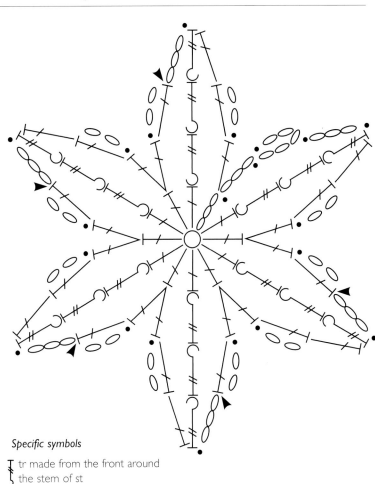

Specific symbols

⊤ tr made from the front around
⌠ the stem of st

⊤ tr made from the back around
⌡ the stem of st

79 SNOWFLAKES
directory view pages 42 and 43

Yarn 4-ply-weight crochet yarn in white and silver metallic
Extras White PVA craft glue, cork mat or bulletin board covered with polyethylene, rustproof pins

METHOD

LARGE SNOWFLAKE
Make 5ch, join with ss into a ring.
1st round (RS) 1ch, [1sc in ring, 10ch] 6 times, ss in first sc.
6 loops.
2nd round Ss in each of first 2ch of next 10-ch sp,
(1ch, 1sc, 3ch, 2sc, 5ch, 2sc, 3ch, 1sc) in same ch sp,
[2ch, (1sc, 3ch, 2sc, 5ch, 2sc, 3ch, 1sc) in next 10-ch sp]
5 times, 2ch, ss in first sc.
3rd round Ss in next 3-ch sp, 1ch, 1sc in same ch sp,
[11ch, miss next 5-ch sp, 1sc in next 3-ch sp, 3ch, 1sc in
next 3-ch sp] 5 times, 11ch, miss next 5-ch sp, 1sc in next
3-ch sp, 3ch, ss in first sc.
4th round [Ss in each of first 6ch of next 11-ch loop, 6ch,
miss 1ch, ss in each of next 3ch, 4ch, miss 1ch, ss in
each of next 2ch, 4ch, miss 1ch, ss in each of next
3ch, 3ch, miss 1ch, ss in each of next 3ch, 4ch,
miss 1ch, ss in each of next 5ch, ss in ch already
worked into, ss in each of remaining 5ch of
11-ch loop, 1sc in sc, 7ch, miss 1ch, ss in each of
next 3ch, 3ch, 1sc in next sc] 6 times, ending ss in
first ss.

SMALL SNOWFLAKE
Make 6ch, join with ss into a ring.
1st round (RS) 6ch, [1tr in ring, 2ch] 11 times, ss in
4th ch of 6ch. 12 ch sp.
2nd round 1ch, 1sc in same st below, 2sc in next ch sp,
1sc in next tr, [5ch, miss next ch sp, 1sc in next tr, 2sc in
next ch sp, 1sc in next tr] 5 times, 5ch, ss in first sc.
3rd round Ss in next sc, 1ch, sc decrease in ss below and
next sc, [5ch, 1dc in next 5-ch sp, 5ch, miss 1sc, sc decrease
in next 2sc] 5 times, 5ch, 1dc in next 5-ch sp, 5ch, ss in top
of first sc decrease.
4th round 1ch, 1sc in same st below, [(3sc, picot, 3sc) in
next 5-ch sp, 1sc in next dc, 4ch, 3 picot, ss in each of 4ch,
1sc in dc, (3sc, picot, 3sc) in next 5-ch sp] 6 times, ending
ss in first sc.

Specific stitch **picot** 3ch, miss 2ch, ss in next ch.

LARGE SNOWFLAKE

FINISHING Dilute 2 tablespoons of white PVA craft glue in 3½fl oz (100ml) of cold water. Soak finished snowflakes in this solution for about 10 minutes. Remove from solution, gently squeeze out excess liquid, and place snowflake upside down on a cork mat (or bulletin board) covered with polyethylene. Carefully ease each snowflake into shape, pinning out the points with rustproof pins. Allow to dry completely before removing pins—this can take 24 hours.

SMALL SNOWFLAKE

PROJECTS

You will probably have decided how you would like to use the designs that appeal to you the most. But, if you haven't, here are some suggestions for brightening, enlivening, or just having fun adorning clothes, household objects, or gifts.

PROJECT 1: SPECIMEN BUTTERFLIES

Much kinder than displaying real butterflies is to make your own.
First choose your colors and paint a second-hand box frame. Stiffen
the butterfly with card, glue it to slices of wine-bottle cork, then
glue these to the background card and insert it into the frame.

PROJECT 2: STRAW HAT

No-one will mistake this gigantic bumble-bee for the real thing, but he makes an amusing addition to a vintage summer hat. He's attached by running a short length of wire through his underside, pushing the ends through the straw hat and twisting them together on the inside.

PROJECT 3: TEA COZY

This sprig of olives would make an elegant corsage, but here it's used as a decorative addition to a plain old-fashioned tea cozy. The stem is simply tucked into the cord at the top so that it can be removed when the cozy needs to be washed.

PROJECT 4: CORAL NECKLACE

Jumbo-sized knitted coral and outsize fake pearl beads are a
frivolous take on traditional jewelry, although finer yarn could
be used for a daintier result. Using a sharp-pointed needle,
the coral and beads were strung on strong thread, and the
ends stitched to organza ribbon, folded in the middle.

PROJECT 5: GOLDFISH

Instead of keeping a live fish in an aquarium, suspend a sequinned crochet goldfish in a kitchen jar to decorate a child's room. "Invisible" nylon sewing thread tied to a twig across the top of the jar keeps the fish dangling happily—and there's no water required!

PROJECT 6: FALL COLORS

Liven up an old tweed jacket with an array of autumnal leaves and mushrooms. They're just the thing to wear when tramping through the woods and foraging for real fungi. A few carefully placed stitches will keep them in place better than pins.

PROJECT 7: CHRISTMAS DOVE

A dove of peace is particularly appropriate at this season. Here, she sits happily among the baubles on a Christmas wreath, but she could be wired to a branch of evergreen, or even top the Christmas tree itself.

INDEX

RESOURCES

YARN SUPPLIERS

Debbie Bliss
Knitting Fever Inc.
315 Bayview Avenue
Amityville
New York 11701
tel: 00 1 516 546 3600
web: www.knittingfever.com

Rowan and Jaeger Yarns Distributor
Rowan c/o Westminster Fibers
165 Ledge Street
Nashua NH 03063
web: www.westminsterfibers.com

WEBSITES

Many other yarn suppliers and useful information can be found on the internet. These are just a few websites:

www.brownsheep.com
www.coatsandclark.com
www.dmc.com
www.knitrowan.com
www.knittingabout.com
www.theyarnco.com
www.yarnsinternational.com

CREDITS

I would like to thank Jan Eaton and Caroline Sullivan for the designs they contributed, Susan Horan for checking the instructions, Simon Pask and Lizzie Orme for their photography, and everyone at Quarto for their help and their great encouragement.